CONTENTS

1)	Introduction to Alexander Solzhenitsyn	1
2)	One Day In The Life Of Ivan Denisovich	39
3)	Language and Style, Translation	80
4)	Bibliography	89

BRIGHT NOTES

ONE DAY IN THE LIFE OF IVAN DENISOVICH BY ALEXANDER SOLZHENITSYN

Intelligent Education

Nashville, Tennessee

BRIGHT NOTES: One Day in the Life of Ivan Denisovich
www.BrightNotes.com

No part of this publication may be used or reproduced in any manner whatsoever without written permission, except in the case of brief quotations in critical articles and reviews. For permissions, contact Influence Publishers http://www.influencepublishers.com.

ISBN: 978-1-645420-12-5 (Paperback)
ISBN: 978-1-645420-13-2 (eBook)

Published in accordance with the U.S. Copyright Office Orphan Works and Mass Digitization report of the register of copyrights, June 2015.

Originally published by Monarch Press.
Alexander Solzhenitsyn, 1976
2020 Edition published by Influence Publishers.

Interior design by Lapiz Digital Services. Cover Design by Thinkpen Designs.

Printed in the United States of America.

Library of Congress Cataloging-in-Publication Data forthcoming.
Names: Intelligent Education
Title: BRIGHT NOTES: One Day in the Life of Ivan Denisovich
Subject: STU004000 STUDY AIDS / Book Notes

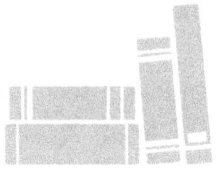

INTRODUCTION TO ALEXANDER SOLZHENITSYN

"For the ethical force with which he has pursued the indispensable traditions of Russian literature." - From the Nobel Prize Citation for Alexander Solzhenitsyn, October 8, 1970.

In mid-century - 1962 to be exact - a bright new talent appeared with stunning suddenness on the literary horizon. Alexander Solzhenitsyn, together with his epoch-making work, *One Day In The Life Of Ivan Denisovich*, flared up like a supernova in the Eastern skies and incandesced the Western skies as well. Today Solzhenitsyn remains the most impressive figure in world literature of the latter half of the 20th century.

Before *One Day* was throttled in the USSR, it had become an overnight sensation. The 100,000 copies of *Novy Mir* (*New World*) carrying the novella sold out in November 1962 in a matter of hours; so did the almost 1 million copies of immediate second and third printings. But by 1963, not only Solzhenitsyn, who had earlier been a protege of the Soviet leader Nikita Khrushchev, but Khrushchev himself fell under a cloud as a new wave of political and cultural Reactionism again loomed in the Soviet Union. By the end of 1964, the editor of *Novy Mir* (Tvardovsky), Khrushchev, Solzhenitsyn, and a number of other liberal elements or influences in Soviet culture became the targets of a widening campaign to restore Stalinist orthodoxy and a rigid party line to the arts.

Nineteen sixty-two, debut year for *One Day In The Life Of Ivan Denisovich* and its author, was an important **episode** in the most unusual, if brief, epoch in recent Soviet history. This was the time-1961-1962-of crisscrossing, incongruous developments, both in domestic as well as foreign policy.

CONDEMNATION OF STALINISM

On the Soviet home scene, the De-Stalinization Campaign reached a crescendo. Stalin's embalmed body, which lay next to Lenin's, was abruptly removed from the Lenin Mausoleum on the party's orders and reinterred in a humble plot at the foot of the Kremlin Wall. This action became a potent symbol of the widening condemnation of Stalin's draconic policies with respect to other party comrades, the arts, and the population at large. In the arts, the liberals now sought to make new inroads, to come out of the closet and with them, their manuscripts out of desk drawers. This process was illustrated by the liberal poets Yevgeny Yevtushenko and Andrei Voznesensky, and other writers acquiring new posts in writers' unions and on editorial boards of journals. "The younger generation of Russians," Yevtushenko announced confidently during a lecture tour to England in May 1962, "are increasingly beginning to feel themselves masters in their own country." The liberal journal *Yunost'* (*Youth*) published Vasily Aksenov's trailblazing story "A Ticket to the Stars" while a heterodoxical work also published in *Yunost's* pages (each issue of which sold like hot pirozhkis) was that a youthful rebellion of sorts was underway in the USSR, that younger people were becoming outspokenly critical of the values and policies identified with the older. Stalinist generation.

Such heretical works and attitudes by no means were left unchallenged by the conservatives and hardliners attached to the regime. In fact, 1962 and 1963 represented the beginnings of an effort, culminating in the mid-1970s, to clamp down on the liberal tendencies that were in such evidence during these years and upon whose crests Solzhenitsyn and *One Day* rode to prominence. One of the signs that a crackdown was imminent was barely concealed (by Aesopian language) in Yevtushenko's sensational poem published during the Cuban Missile Crisis week in October 1962 entitled, "The Heirs of Stalin." In this short but trenchant political poem (which, incidentally, was printed in the party daily *Pravda*, edited at the time by Khrushchev allies), Yevtushenko warned against the possible recrudescence of Stalinism in his country. "A telephone line is installed [in Stalin's coffin]," he wrote. "Stalin has not given up," his "telephone line" runs all the way to Communist reactionaries in Tirana (Albania), Peking, and to the Kremlin. The poem concludes: "As long as Stalin's heirs exist on earth/It will seem to me/That Stalin is still in the Mausoleum."

Yevtushenko's warning of a political rollback began to take on concrete meaning at the end of 1962, after publication of *One Day*, and especially in the spring of 1963. First came the Cuban Missile Crisis, or what came to be called for the Soviets the "Cuban fiasco." Soviet merchantmen bound for Havana with lethal missiles lashed to their decks were turned back in humiliating U-shaped wakes-a retreat forced on the Russians by a U.S. naval blockade ordered from the White House by President John F. Kennedy. Kremlin watchers immediately detected slippage in Khrushchev's standing in the Moscow leadership; Soviet lossof-face became obvious to hundreds of millions of newspaper readers throughout the world.

The second straw-that-broke-Nikita's-back was the embarrassing exposure found in the notorious *Penkovsky Papers*. Col. Oleg Penkovsky had been a deputy chief of a department in the hush-hush State Committee for Coordinating Scientific Research and probably, too, a member of Soviet military intelligence. In October 1962 he was arrested in Moscow for having acted as a double agent, for the USSR but also for both the U.S. and U.K. intelligence services. Needless to say, he was executed, in somewhere like the basement of Lubyanka prison, but not without leaving behind in the West his papers, which then became available to Western media. *The Penkovsky Papers* told a story of slack discipline among Soviet intelligence agents (not to mention the treason of Penkovsky himself), revealed the names of secret agents and their means of conducting espionage in the West, and seemed to illustrate a general laxity which, to the conservatives, had been brought on by Khrushchev-endorsed policies of liberalization.

Third, there was the poor showing of the Soviet economy, according to the fourth-quarter 1962 economic report; the crucial sector of agriculture was especially shortfallen.

Encouraged by these and other turns of events as the year 1963 opened, the Kremlin hardliners, joined by the culture hawks, were loaded for bear. Khrushchev, his liberal-minded son-in-law (Adzhubei), and a whole flock of liberal-lining authors and critics came under the sights of the reactionaries. The list of dramatis personae in this unfolding drama to unseat the First Secretary and to turn back the clock on the Soviet cultural scene is too long to recount here; in any case, it is the results that speak just as loud as the step-by-step causal chain which brought them about.

SOLZHENITSYN ATTACKED

The blips of reaction were clearly manifest at the turn of the year 1962. The Soviet super-patriotic, party-lining author and critic, Nikolai Gribachev, aimed a stinging attack against Yevtushenko in the pages of *Pravda* in January 1963. Ilya Ehrenburg, one of the more respected of old generation liberals, author of the pace-setting novel of 1953, ironically titled *The Thaw*, was raked over the coals in the government daily Izvestiya. In these and other party-initiated criticisms, the message was that the cultural expression of de-Stalinization must be halted. Moreover, there was the implication that de-Stalinization as a whole, not only in the arts, should be discontinued. liberal journals - *Yunost'* and *Novy Mir* particularly - came under sharp attack. One Lydia Fomenko attacked both Solzhenitsyn and the magazine that had carried *One Day in the Life of Ivan Denisovich* (for showing a lack of "philosophical perspective"); socialism, she wrote, was built in the Soviet Union, and along with it the various Stalinist institutions, quite aside from and despite the fact of Stalin's "personal short-comings" (!). It was profoundly mistaken, she maintained, to identify socialism with Stalin, as Solzhenitsyn had done implicitly in *One Day*.

Nikita Khrushchev himself felt obliged to join the swelling chorus of straight-laced neo-Stalinists on the cultural front. Whether he was under duress or not, the First Secretary took out after Ehrenburg and Yevtushenko, and Viktor Nekrasov, all of whose modest literary heresies he had apparently once tolerated, perhaps even encouraged, to further his own political ends. Now Khrushchev talked the language of the conservatives: "Our Soviet youth," the Leader reminded his audience at a special Kremlin conference of 600 writers, artists, and intellectuals in March 1963, "has been brought up by our party; it follows our party; and it sees in it its educator and leader." Harangued on the rostrum by the party apparatchik Leonid Ilyichev and other spokesmen for a hard line on the arts, this conference heard one orthodox-minded speaker after another defend the older generation against the younger, while at the same time each denied that any "fathers-and-sons" confrontation or minor generation gap could possibly exist under Soviet conditions. Some, including Khrushchev, held up the example of the author Mikhail Sholokhov, famous for his great novel Quiet Flows the Don (but some, Solzhenitsyn for one, question the authenticity of his authorship of the work) but for precious little else. They pitted this author against the other of his generation, Ehrenburg, in a subtle but nonetheless obvious display of anti-Semitism to prove that the one (Sholokhov) was a genuine revolutionist and Communist while the other (Ehrenburg) was a sham, a coward, even a "silent" collaborator in the foul deeds of Stalin.

The next step - and this, too, was crucial for the careers of *One Day* and its author - was the start of a gradual but steady Rehabilitation Of Stalin. Just as Khrushchev had used the de-Stalinization campaign to embarrass the old Stalinist rivals in his leadership, even to purge some of them as he did in 1957, likewise and anti-Khrushchev forces pushed for Stalin's rehabilitation precisely for the purpose of sandbagging the First Secretary. Some of the most denunciatory of anti-Stalin spokesmen of the recent past (Leonid Brezhnev among them) one-by-one joined the anti-Khrushchev alliance. This was the group of conservatives, a virtual crypto-cabinet, who not only opposed any continuance or broadening of the anti-Stalin campaign, but who also wished to overturn a number of Khrushchev domestic and foreign policies.

The grounds were that these policies were ill-advised, too liberal, or too "hare-brained," as the Central Committee's indictment against Khrushchev put it in October 1964 - that is when the First Secretary was finally replaced by a team of neo-Stalinists headed by Brezhnev, Alexei Kosygin, and Mikhail Suslov.

For *One Day in the Life of Ivan Denisovich*, 1963-1964 was a turning point. In fact, the pressure to rehabilitate Stalin and contain de-Stalinization had an obvious connection with the nomination of *One Day* - and for its failure to win - the Lenin Prize. During the autumn of 1963 and into 1964, literati in Russia discussed the possibility of Solzhenitsyn's receiving the prize for 1964. The Communist youth daily, *Komsomolskaya Pravda*, went so far as to publish a letter to the editor by a reader who recommended that *One Day* get the Lenin Prize for literature. (Several works are customarily nominated for the prize, the final decision being made by an "illustrious" body of judges who are under strong pressure from the party.) The same newspaper, answering as it were the reader's letter, criticized the behavior of the novella's main character, the prisoner, Ivan Shukhov, for being "distasteful." Another Solzhenitsyn writing which figured in the pre-prize discussion was *Matryona's Place*, a story published in *Novy Mir* shortly after *One Day*. In the discussion, the "pros" seemed outnumbered, at least by their connections, by the "cons" on the matter of whether Solzhenitsyn should receive the prize. Finally, in February 1964 a joint meeting of the secretariats (which are customarily saturated with partiytsi [party-liners]) of the RSFSR and Moscow writers' organizations determined that *One Day* "cannot be placed among the outstanding works which are worthy of the Lenin Prize." A bitterly ironic remark began to circulate around Moscow after this, to many people, shocking rejection of *One Day*: "Tell me what you think of *One Day* and I will proceed to tell you just who you are."

Once the Brezhnev-Kosygin-Suslov triumvirate (Podgorny, the "Soviet President," might be counted to make it a quadrumvirate, except that many observers take this official's family name quite seriously - it means "foothills") was in power, a series of occurrences, obviously launched directly from the Kremlin, foreshadowed neo-Stalinism on the cultural front.

First came the Brodsky Case of February 1965. Brodsky, a writer, was accused of being a "parasite" and a few other things. Above all, it was his "anti-Soviet" verses which provoked the State Prosecutor's various "witnesses" into such remarks as describing Brodsky's (or any writer's) mind as a "dangerous weapon." Another said, "Brodsky has torn our youth away from its work, from the world and from life" and, "Brodsky has played a great anti-social role." The court sentenced the writer to five years in an Archangel (near the Arctic Circle in north-western European Russia) forced labor camp. His job: carting manure. This was the price paid by a Russian poet who had been "guilty" of writing an **elegy** to John Donne and some other somewhat mystical, religious, or lyrical verses, most of them considered outstanding by Western critics for their cadences and symbolism. The Brodsky Trial became a minor sensation among Western (and also certain Yugoslav) literati, and among those Soviet intellectuals who were knowledgeable about both Brodsky and the star-chamber-like proceedings against him. Even some fellow-traveler critics in the West found it hard to justify the sentencing of the poet. Other observers thought the regime was over-reacting both to the short spell of liberalization under Khrushchev, and to such phenomena as the public disorders in the Soviet cities of Ryazan, Novocherkassk, Omsk, Odessa, Krivoi Rog, and elsewhere in the early 1960s. Moreover, the worldwide "youth rebellion," typified by Beatlemania, could prove, and already seemed to be proving, subversive to Soviet official conceptions of party and state authoritarianism.

SOLZHENITSYN NOVELS REJECTED

As the news of other trials and repressions against writers began to reach the West, Alexander Solzhenitsyn began to figure in the tightening reins being placed over the arts by the post-Khrushchev rulers. The heyday of the Khrushchev years was over, that former time of thaw when the First Secretary personally had introduced the author to several top leaders in the Kremlin and when Khrushchev single-handedly gave the green light to the publication of *One Day*. Solzhenitsyn and his hundreds of thousands of appreciative readers had to endure the humiliation of seeing the 1964 Lenin Prize go to a third-rate novelist named Oleg Gonchar. Moreover, the two new Solzhenitsyn works, *The First Circle* and *Cancer Ward*, could not be published in the USSR, despite pressure from the influential *Novy Mir* editor, Alexander Tvardovsky. In the case of the latter novel, Tvardovsky's magazine had actually prepared the first eight chapters for the composing room only to have the permission from on high to publish delayed time after time, much to *Novy Mir* readers' dismay and perplexity. Eventually, of course, *Cancer Ward* did surface, in the West; that destroyed whatever slim chance the work ever had of being published in the Soviet Union.

Out of these reassertions of party and government censorship and "commanding" of the arts, Solzhenitsyn not only emerged bruised but extremely bitter. Solzhenitsyn's already declining standing with the post-K leadership sank even lower. Enter the K.G.B. (the initials standing for Committee on State Security, or Komitet Gosudarstvennoi Bezopasnosti). Came the confiscations of manuscripts in the apartment of a friend of the author's. Solzhenitsyn countered by circulating his forbidden writings in the form of carbon typescripts on the circuit known as samizdat, or do-it-yourself publishing.

The next stage in Solzhenitsyn's worsening relations with the regime - and the tempering of his own attitude toward it- came on the occasion of the convocation of the Fourth Congress of the Union of Writers. This conference, which had been much postponed (a sure sign of disarray), was convened against the backdrop of arrests, trials, harsh sentences to camps, and commitment to mental institutions of intellectuals guilty only of idea-heresy. (For a full description of this emerging pattern of regime repression and the deepening and broadening of anti-Soviet dissidence in the USSR, see Albert L. Weeks, *Andrei Sakharov And The Soviet Dissidents*, Monarch Notes, 1975.) In a fighting mood, the author prepared 250 copies of a letter which he had addressed to the delegates to the congress. Copies of this fascinating document reached periodicals in the West, among them the Op-Ed Department of *The New York Times, Le Monde*, and other European publications.

SOLZHENITSYN CHALLENGES CENSORSHIP

Solzhenitsyn proposed an ingenious addition to the officially-approved congress agenda, that the delegates openly discuss Censorship of Literature in the USSR. Wrote the author: "/Censorship/is a survival of the Middle Ages." How has censorship managed, he asked, "to remain alive Methuselah-like" already on the eve of the 21st century? Solzhenitsyn went on to list those authors of the Tsarist past who had been censored in their day, Dostoyevsky among them, and to the many more authors whose pens were stilled under Lenin and Stalin (by what Pasternak called the "Komissarocracy"): Yesenin, Akhmatova, Mandelshtam, Bulgakov, Tsvetayeva, Zoshchenko, Pilnyak, Babel, Pasternak, et al. Solzhenitsyn then told the delegates (though, of course, only a few ever saw his letter but many heard of its contents) that the writer's union by-laws should be rewritten so as to protect members from regime interference. Then, the author told of his own frustrating experience, with attempting to get *The First Circle*, among other writings, published in the USSR (whose Constitution guarantees freedom of the press, publishing, etc.). He also related how the Soviet government had prevented him from appearing before the public, to read from his work, give lectures, etc. Finally, he closed his letter with these moving words: "I am of course confident that I will fulfill my duty as a writer under any circumstances-from the grave even more successfully and more undeniably than during my own lifetime. No one can bar the road to truth, and to advance its cause I am prepared to accept even death."

Those who were able to obtain a copy of Solzhenitsyn's letter, and even those who were not, began to express their appreciation for the author's frankness and bravery. One of these responses took the form of an open letter signed by no less than 80 members of the writer's union, some of them delegates to the congress itself. In all, nearly 100 writers declared their support for the letter. Some well-known names of Soviet literati were on the list of the 80-among them, Paustovsky, Kaverin, Tendryakov, Voinovich and Aksenov.

The next move by Solzhenitsyn was to send a second letter to the writer's union secretariat. He protested that although a great number of writers had voiced their support of the first letter's contents, it had neither been published in the USSR nor answered by the officials to whom it had been sent. He further pointed out that *One Day in the Life of Ivan Denisovich* was being secretly withdrawn from Soviet libraries, while readers were not infrequently being warned not even to lend *One Day* to anyone let alone give it to another person. Moreover, the author warned that *Cancer Ward* had already begun to leak to the West, its eventual appearance in toto "cannot be prevented."

Finally, a response did come - to Letter No.2. Solzhenitsyn was called before a meeting of the board of the writer's union - this was in September 1967. It was an unequal confrontation between the author, who was acting in his own behalf, and a panel of cultural bureaucrats who sharply attacked him for his alleged "nonconformity," for being a "leader of political opposition in our country," for not protesting the "dirty use of your name by our enemies in the West." Solzhenitsyn met his attackers with an angry counterattack, the partial text of which may be read in a book by a Soviet dissident named Pavel Litvinov, *The Demonstration in Pushkin Square* (see Albert L. Weeks, *Andrei Sakharov And The Soviet Dissidents*, Monarch Notes pp. 9-10; 52-3). What most disturbed him, he told this mini-Red Star-Chamber proceeding, was the "destiny of our great literature, which once conquered and captivated the world but which has now lost its standing." A party-lining cultural hawk who was in attendance at the confrontation (Anatoly Surkov) remarked significantly that "the works of Solzhenitsyn are more dangerous to us than those of Pasternak." [Note: Pasternak, author of Doctor Zhivago, a work which was never permitted to be published in the USSR.] Moreover, Surkov went on, "while Pasternak was a man divorced from life, Solzhenitsyn ... is a man of principle."

Subsequent to his appearance before the writers' union secretariat (but also to a somewhat lesser degree earlier), Solzhenitsyn was attacked by name in various party-approved articles in the daily press and in periodicals. In a note to Solzhenitsyn from the writers' union secretariat, the author was asked if he wished to "reconsider" his position, perhaps issue a "public statement delineating your position on the anti-Soviet campaign involving your name." Solzhenitsyn answered this note by firing back eight questions of his own. Most of them were reiterations of his recommendations made in the letter to the Fourth Congress of Writers; all of them were cast in that candid style that is so familiar to the readers of Solzhenitsyn's prose, especially as found in his various unanswered letters to Soviet officials.

WORLDWIDE REPUTATION

By 1968, Solzhenitsyn's name was so well known abroad, not to mention in his own country, that his former editor at *Novy Mir*, the ailing Alexander Tvardovsky, could speak of Solzhenitsyn's acquisition of a "worldwide reputation." But, Tvardovsky went on to say in the letter to Fedin, First Secretary of the Writers' Union, the "literary temptations of the West are completely alien [to Solzhenitsyn]." In no way could the author be accused of "placating" the West, Tvardovsky said. The year 1968 not only marked the increased severity of the officially-approved public attacks on the author but also a stepping up of the dissident movement inside the USSR. The sudden invasion and occupation of "fraternal Czechoslovakia" by Soviet-led troops of Moscow's closet East European allies in August 1968 gave an added boost to the anti-regime feelings among significant portions of the Soviet intelligentsia. It was precisely at this point, too, that Solzhenitsyn began to associate himself with increasing frequency with the various dissident causes which arose over arrests, trials, and sentencings of other intellectuals. Not surprisingly, the author was at last expelled (November 1969) from his own writers' union in Ryazan - the charge was that he had written "anti-Soviet books." Solzhenitsyn's reply was: "[Your] hatred is no better than racial hatred ... [it has become] your sterile atmosphere."

"SOLZH"

For about a year following his expulsion from the Ryazan writers' union, little was heard about Solzhenitsyn. Then, with the same meteoric suddenness with which the reading public had first come to know the author's name at the time of the appearance of *One Day in the Life of Ivan Denisovich*, the news from Stockholm in October 1970 was that Alexander Isayevich Solzhenitsyn had been awarded the Nobel Prize for Literature. Newspapers in the non-Communist world, and a few in the Communist world too, carried the news item prominently in their pages. (The *New York Daily News*, a tabloid with a huge circulation but with too little room for long names, used an abbreviated form of Solzhenitsyn's name -"SOLZH" - most readers presumably knowing to whom the newspaper referred. Solzhenitsyn himself sometimes signs his name this way.)

This momentous development recalled a previous occasion when the Nobel Prize was awarded to a controversial Russian author - the case of Pasternak in 1958. At that time, the author of Doctor Zhivago declined the award, remarking that he had done so because of the "significance" that has been imparted to it "in the society to which I belong." Although he had turned down the award, vitriolic attacks on Pasternak went so far as to demand that the author renounce his citizenship. Subsequent statements by Pasternak were sadly self-humiliating and apologetic. Appeals in the author's defense came from well-known literary figures the world over, among them J. B. Priestley, Graham Greene, Bertrand Russell, and a Communist writer or two. (Boris Pasternak died of cancer of the stomach on May 30, 1960, a man broken in body, wounded in spirit, whose burial at Peredelkino on the outskirts of Moscow was attended by several thousand people who were closely observed by over 100 K.G.B. plainclothesmen). Now, some 10 years later as a second controversial Russian author was again awarded the Nobel Prize, how would he, Solzhenitsyn, react?

Swiftly. Solzhenitsyn made public a statement in which he unhesitatingly affirmed his acceptance of the award, "as far as it depends on me." So also did the Soviet press respond speedily. Izvestiya ran a statement by the writers' union which deplored the giving of the award to Solzhenitsyn, calling it a politically hostile action. It was clear that, despite Solzhenitsyn's own acceptance of the award, the author would not be permitted to leave the country, to go to Sweden personally to receive the prize at the awarding ceremonies. The ceremonies went on without Solzhenitsyn, but not without a short Solzhenitsyn message being read to the Nobel Prize festival at Stockholm's city hall. This message was delivered by Dr. Karl-Ragnar Gierow on December 10, 1970. Dr. Gierow's own panegyric on Solzhenitsyn's contribution to world literature was stunning. Among other things, the Permanent Secretary of the Swedish Academy said of the author: "Solzhenitsyn is of the incomparable Russian tradition ... [of] the gigantic predecessors who have derived from Russia's suffering the compelling strength and inextinguishable love that permeate their work .... When Solzhenitsyn's novel *One Day in the Life of Ivan Denisovich* first appeared eight years ago, it was recognized at once in his own country and soon all over the world that a new writer had entered the arena." Finally, in describing the manner in which the author present a single day in the life of a prisoner in a Stalinist labor camp, Dr. Gierow said: "The narrative focuses on the only human element in existence, the human individual ... one destiny among millions and a million destinies in one. This is the whole of humanism in a nutshell, for the kernel is love of mankind. This year's Nobel Prize for Literature has been awarded to the proclaimer of such a humanism." The Nobel Prize-winner himself was unable to hear these words of praise but had to read about them in the Western press, or possibly hear them over foreign radio (e.g., on Radio Liberty out of Munich or the Voice of America). Sholokhov, when he received the same award in 1965, had of course been permitted to travel to Stockholm. Sholokhov is the kind of Soviet author who pays servile homage to the powers-that-be in the Kremlin; he can go anywhere.

DISPUTE OVER "G" IN GOD

It looked to many in the West as if the Brezhnev-Kosygin regime might pin an arrestable offense on Solzhenitsyn, thus ridding the Soviet literary as well as dissident scene of a "troublemaker," and an increasingly famous one at that. But the Kremlin took no action, at least not at that time (1970-1). Instead, it kept the eyes of the K.G.B. on the author, agents occasionally following him about Moscow. Meanwhile, the author took the major turn in his literary career of undertaking the writing of a trilogy of history-oriented books, starting with *August 1914*. Needless to say, every one of the state publishing houses to which Solzhenitsyn submitted *August 1914* turned it down (as they had countless other manuscripts, including *Cancer Ward*). Undaunted, the author openly contacted the Paris-based Russian literature publisher, the YMCA Press. In writing to this publisher, Solzhenitsyn noted that one of the reasons why Soviet publishers had rejected *August 1914* was that the word God bore a capital G. This censorious intrusion, wrote the author, is "unintelligible to normal human reason ... The directive to write God in small letters is the cheapest kind of atheistic pettiness." When the word God appeared in the *Novy Mir* Russian original of *One Day*, it was written with a lower-case g-perhaps the pound of flesh paid to the Soviet censor as part of the arrangement for publishing *One Day*.

August 1914, finally published in the West by well-known publishers, was "volume one" and the first in a cycle of writings on which Solzhenitsyn is presently working and which tell the story of the immediate prelude to the revolutionary events of 1917 culminating in the Bolshevik seizure of power on November 7, 1917.

DEFINES "TRUE LITERATURE"

Solzhenitsyn's turning to history has extremely important consequences for his total literary heritage. As he himself has said, "Literature that is not the very breath of contemporary society does not deserve the name of literature." To be true literature, "the pain and fears of society must be held before it, society must be warned against the moral and social dangers which threaten it."

History to Solzhenitsyn, as to Leo Tolstoy, is the theater and the arena in which the abominations as well as the glories of human behavior are revealed at their most powerful and on the grandest scale. This is not to say that Solzhenitsyn actually "writes history," meaning by that a formal history text. Rather, his novel *August 1914* is a vehicle for the telling the larger story of the human condition. As in *One Day*, characters are minutely inspected in order best to understand the historical environment in which they participate as well as being affected by it. In other words, history at its present juncture provides Solzhenitsyn with concrete, "living" referents or the actual background against which the moral fiber of realistically depicted characters are not only revealed but above all tested and tempered. As in the later work, *Gulag Archipelago*, Solzhenitsyn's historical novel about Leninist-Stalinist terror and the labor-camp system, so in *August 1914* events do not simply "happen," as though they were products of the action of Fate. It is precisely over the issue of Why Events Happen that Solzhenitsyn parts company with the great Russian writer, Tolstoy, who himself used history (*War and Peace*) as a means of dissecting the human spirit and human character.

For Solzhenitsyn, the tragedies of individual men and women-say, as found in forced labor camps-are not decreed by Fate or by heaven. These individual tragedies are seen as parts, packets, or "knots" (uzly, Solzhenitsyn's term) of a larger Tragedy, capital T. People are often seen as victims of institutionalized distortions of humanity-whether such institutions be Lenin's revolutionary tribunals, Leninist-Stalinist censorship, or the *Gulag Archipelago*. But note that the institutions themselves which debase the victims are not the inexorable result of "historical necessity." Such institutions are not only avoidable, but the author strongly implies, eradicable, even though they have become deeply entrenched as, for example, in Soviet society.

Not that Solzhenitsyn is a "revolutionary," in the usual sense of that word. Indeed, he could never dedicate himself to revolution, implying as it does the unleashing of violence and of "vranyo" (Russian for deceitful ballyhoo and propaganda), of paying servile homage to cults, either of leaders, ideologies, or of the State and the Party. Such particular "Causes" or "The Cause" frequently disappoint and disillusion their followers (as happened on a small scale as described by John Simon Kunen in The Strawberry Statement, for example), despite their pious-sounding goals and alleged "self-transcending devotion."

Solzhenitsyn is tuned in on a more distant, yet more proximate drummer: his Muse. As an artist, his metier is the calling up of vivid images, even when he is retelling the history of twentieth-century Russia. At all times it is the stark, unadorned reality of the world, and of the people living in it, which interest Solzhenitsyn. But as he tells of the results of the foregoing events, of the decisions and personalities (including Tsar Nicholas I, his ministers and generals, Lenin, Stalin, et al.) participating in history, Solzhenitsyn also seeks out the causes (causation) which have brought about the historical consequences. Most of the major actions occurring in history, as Solzhenitsyn views it, are due to conscious human initiation motivated by consciously defined purposes.

In short, Solzhenitsyn's Sense Of Tragedy is distinctly non-classical as well as non-Tolstoyan. Heroic characters are not "tragically-flawed" or innocent victims of unconscious or unknowable forces or enigmas. Solzhenitsyn's is faintly Manichaean viewpoint, in which the world and the historical terrain are populated with persons-whether at the grassroots or at the very summit of power-who appear to be intrinsically, almost genetically, either evil or on the other hand, good. For Solzhenitsyn, there are demonic natures and humanitarian natures. To him, the evil-doers may outnumber the benefactors of mankind, at least in contemporary political and social life, but they do not ultimately defeat them. This view is not only non-classical, it is also non-nineteenth century. In the preceding century, more times than not, history was viewed, whether by trained historians or by the writers of fiction and philosophy, as a "process." It could be studied "scientifically" as though it were an environment resembling the Galapagos Islands where Darwin studied natural processes. Indeed, to the nineteenth-century historian, history was often viewed as a law-bound evolution. Terms such as "process," "historicism," "determinism," "impersonal forces," "inevitability," etc., were employed to give scientific-better, scientistic-credence to the telling of history. In What is History? Edward Hallett Carr has called this tendency in historiography a misunderstanding of the nature of science (whether natural science or social science), the failure to appreciate that historians advance "progressively from one fragmentary hypothesis to another," not by means of dogmatic insistence upon "historical law" and "ultimate truth."

So, for Solzhenitsyn, man's Tragedy does not consist in his being ground under by an historical juggernaut, a dumb force guided by inexorable historical laws, impersonal forces, economic determinism, and so forth. Instead, man makes his own history. Ideologies, religions, policies do help shape the lines along which history will be made, but above all for Solzhenitsyn, it is men who make history. It is they who can be blamed. So can the makers of ideologies be blamed for the postulates they develop and the consequences which result from them. "Who is to blame?" the author of *Gulag Archipelago* asks in the chapter entitled, "The Law Becomes a Man." He answers, with bitter **irony**: "Well, of course, it obviously could never be the Over-All Leadership!"

LIFE

Isai Solzhenitsyn, the father of Alexander, was a pacifist until his country found itself at war (World War I) with the Central Powers led by Germany. The spontaneous patriotism set off by the conflict enveloped the whole nation, and the Solzhenitsyn family in particular. Isai, a philology student, answered the call to arms and distinguished himself as an artillery officer on the Eastern Front, where he was decorated three times for bravery under fire.

In 1917, the year of the several revolutionary outbursts led off by the abdication of the Tsar, Isai married an idealistic, "progressive" young woman who was well educated and with a strong interest in literature and the arts. (The marriage ceremony was performed right on the battlefield, by a combat chaplain.)

Once the war was over and the soldiers demobilized, Isai and his bride settled in Kislovodsk in southwestern Russia where the foothills of the Caucasus Mountains begin their gradual rise to the peaks which border on the Near East. It was good stag and boar country, and one day, when Isai was on a hunt, his rifle discharged by accident, wounding him fatally. Six months after his death, Alexander was born-December 11, 1918.

A more tumultuous time to be born in Russia one cannot imagine. The bloody Civil War (whose victims were eventually to number 3 million) was underway, with Whites fighting Reds and Greens fighting Reds, while a makeshift expeditionary force, consisting of British, Americans, and others who had attempted to guard stores of military supplies during the war and after the Bolsheviks captured power in November 1917, also participated in the anti-Bolshevik struggle.

Needless to say, Alexander's mother belonged to the "class enemy," since she was of middle-class origins; finding work was difficult. She made the decision to move herself and her son to Rostov-on-Don, not far from Kisovodsk, and found employment there as a freelance typist. Life was extremely difficult for the pair, what with poor diet, her long working hours, and her somewhat fragile physical constitution. Among her poorly-heated and essentially inadequate abodes were ramshackle, thatched-roof izby (huts), even a stable, lacking such essentials as running water or heat, other than from coal which the mother had to carry over long hikes outside of town. Frequent bouts with respiratory infections shortened her life; she died in 1944.

"BOY INTELLECTUAL" HELPS OUT

Not surprisingly, the young son, Alexander, learned to pitch in and help his mother. Despite his constant journeying to search for coal or wood or to earn extra money by this or that chore, the "boy intellectual" found time to engage in deep reading and studying. Probably, the slender blond youth named "Sasha" bore a certain resemblance to a Middle-Western American lad, maybe also his program of self-study and reflection was not unlike Abraham Lincoln's, a man Solzhenitsyn greatly admires. These early years taught him the value of exploiting every minute of free time, of which there was precious little. It also taught him the value of self-discipline, which was to be of such life-saving importance years later when he was to become a real-life Ivan Shukhov spending not "one day," but 8 years in a Stalin labor camp.

When he was at the tender age of 9, he had decided to become a writer, and set about practicing this art. (In this, the young Solzhenitsyn resembles a number of young prodigies of the past who all got early starts-among them, Mozart, Pushkin, Lermontov, et al.) Once he was in the shkola in Rostov, he caught the attention of his teachers because his work in all subjects, but especially in mathematics, was outstanding. His desire to write, his sense of dispassionate and cool observation of the character-types and environment around him-a not uncommon trait in young people who have to fend for themselves-led Alexander to assume a skeptical posture with respect to the growing oppression of Stalinism which he could see all around him. Collectivization - the forcible incorporation of formerly private peasants (whether rich or not, they were referred to by the Kremlin as "kulaks") - caused feelings of revulsion in the young man. (At the summit of power in Moscow, an argument over collectivization between Stalin and his first wife resulted in her suicide in 1932.) Solzhenitsyn thus witnessed and scorned the ladled-out propaganda about Stalin's infallibility, the same Stalin who "liquidated" some 10 million peasant-farmers and who purged and had shot thousands of party workers who were baselessly accused of treason. With the notorious Purge Trials of the 1930s, the total horror of the first totalitarian state in modern times (dating it, as Solzhenitsyn and others say it should be: from November 7, 1917) moved Alexander to "solve the riddle of Stalin."

From this moment on, Solzhenitsyn seems to have dedicated himself to unraveling this riddle, tracing step-by-step how the demonic nature and the power of Stalin distorted and exploited the essentially humanitarian spirit of the Russian nation and character. Even at this early date, while he was still in his teens, Solzhenitsyn embarked on his continuing pursuit of historical documents, the basic truths, the causes of the predicaments and inhuman tragedies which have gripped his beloved country for the past fifty years and before, under the Tsars.

Alexander received a scholarship to attend Rostov University and embarked on a deeper study of his favorite subject of mathematics. And, of course, he continued to write. He was a fascinating blend of a young man who took to natural science and mathematics while possessing a native talent and inclination for belles-lettres. At this time, he was drawn into a circle of friends who were to exert a powerful influence on him. One of these was Nikolai Vitkevich, once a high-school classmate with whom Alexander had played chess and gone hiking, and with whom he had many long "diskussiya" ("bull sessions"). Another was Natalya Reshetovskaya, whom he married in 1940 when both were 21.

CULTIVATING MEMORY

Upon graduation from Rostov University, Solzhenitsyn chose to become a high-school math teacher, although university colleagues had expected that he would go on to do graduate work and research in science In addition to teaching, which he enjoyed immensely, he practiced one of his favorite pastimes, photography. Apparently, his interest in photography was stimulated by his great urge to cultivate the memory - the recording of faces, parts of landscapes, familiar locales and the parts of his physical environment. Among the photographs he still prizes are those of the cupolaed domes of old Russian churches rising over the banks of the Don or the meandering Volga, the "Mississippi" of Russia.

Solzhenitsyn's, and everyone else's, best-laid plans were abruptly interrupted in June 1941 when the Germans launched their surprise attack on Russia. Stalin's pact with Hitler (August 1939) lulled Stalin into inattention to the schemes of the Nazis while Hitler apparently had no intention from the beginning to respect the terms of the Nazi-Soviet Pact, that "agreement among thieves." "Although people did not choose on their own to go to the front, all the keenest and the best people found themselves there," Solzhenitsyn remarked later.

His ill-health (as yet, not clearly specified) disqualified him in the beginning for active military service at the front. So, for the first months after his induction into the Red Army, he acted as stable boy (cavalry and horse transport were not infrequently employed on both the Russian and the German sides, but especially on the former, during the Russo-German phase of World War II). Although it was a safe job, as military assignments went, Solzhenitsyn yearned for front-line duty; it was, after all, part of his nature to engage himself to the fullest extent in whatever he undertook. To know, Solzhenitsyn was fond of pointing out, is to experience, and to experience it first-hand.

CAPTAIN OF ARTILLERY

He got his way. In the middle of 1942, at one of the most critical junctures in the Nazi onslaught which had reached deep into

European Russia, Private Alexander Solzhenitsyn joined an artillery regiment at the front. His agility of mind and facility with mathematics (not to mention his scholarship to the university) helped him win the attention of his commanding officer and eventually a commission as a lieutenant, later, when he was 26, reaching the rank of captain.

His war record was outstanding. He was twice decorated, with the military award of Order of the Red Star and later the much higher award, the Order of the Patriotic War, given to men or women who distinguish themselves with personal valor. An official document on Solzhenitsyn's activities in the thick of battle with the village-by-village defense and advance of the Russian troops toward Germany (west of the city of Orel) 1943-1945 states: "It is clear from 1942 and until his arrest [February 1945], [Captain] Solzhenitsyn remained permanently at the front ... fought courageously for his country, repeatedly displayed personal heroism, and, through his example, inspired the other soldiers in his unit, of which he was in charge. In terms of discipline and merit on the battlefield, [Captain] Solzhenitsyn's battery was the best in his subdivision."

"Until his arrest ..." His passionate feelings about tyranny in his country, the country for which he was prepared to give his life, were bound to catch up with him, even as the war raged on. He and a close friend from former days stationed in a more northern combat zone-let's call him "Lt. X" - exchanged letters with one another on the meaning of the war, its outcome, the postwar future of Russia, etc. Some of what they wrote each other was also recorded in Solzhenitsyn's diary. In their correspondence they raised the sensitive question, "Who was to blame?" for the holocaust of the war, and for the series of events that led up to June 22, 1941? More often than not, they agreed that the root cause was the "cult of Stalin." No wonder, they said, that an anti-Stalin army had formed early in the war (under Gen. Andrei Vlasov) and which joined Hitler's forces in attacking Russia; no wonder millions of Red Army soldiers deserted during the rout in the early months of the war. These were the consequences of the deeply-ingrained hatred felt by so many ordinary Russians for the man they called the "pock-marked devil," or as Solzhenitsyn called him in his purloined letters, "pakhan" (godfather). Despite the fact that both the Captain and "Lt. X" were members of the Communist Party and addressed each other as "Comrade," many of their views were anti-Stalinist, although not yet anti-Leninist.

Solzhenitsyn brought up in his diary any number of grievances which he felt against Stalin and Stalin's personal responsibility for so many personal tragedies of the preceding 15 years. For one thing, he deplored the state of Soviet letters, of literature and the arts. They were downtrodden and made gray by the dictates of party dictatorship and censorship. Stalin's own "literary" adventures were not only crude, wrote Solzhenitsyn, but disgusting; Solzhenitsyn did not lose sight of the fact that Stalin's command of the language was that of a Georgian, for whom Russian was a second language.

"SMERSH"

All mail in the USSR to one extent or another is examined by the censor, sometimes by spot checking, but apparently by examining each and every piece. The military post is especially subjected to this inspection. If a soldier's mail began to assume a certain "complexion" - that is, toward the white end of the spectrum and away from Red - the N.K.V.D's special organization called "SMERSH" (acronym for "Death to Spies" Smert' shpionam) would be brought into the case.

This happened to Captain Solzhenitsyn and his pen-pal, "Lt. X." With Solzhenitsyn at the front near Konigsberg, Prussia, his brigade commander, one Colonel Travkin, informed SMERSH that his accomplished captain would not be available for interrogation, or as it turned out, apprehension, until after the given battle had terminated. The battle at Konigsberg was fierce and it was several days before this key outpost of the German defense was overcome by the Russians. Once he was summoned back to HQ not far from the front, the captain was confronted by a panel of SMERSH agents, his commander, and a Communist "politruk," or political commissar. Solzhenitsyn was asked to hand over his officer's pistol and was thereupon confronted with the charge of having committed a "political crime," punishable under the Criminal Code of the RSFSR and the Military Code as "counterrevolutionary activity." When the inquisition had ended, Captain Solzhenitsyn was placed under arrest, but in a show of respect for his intrepid battery leader and comrade, Colonel Travkin shook Solzhenitsyn's hand-a brave act which Solzhenitsyn was later characteristically to call "one of the most outstanding acts of courage I saw during the war."

Under arrest, Solzhenitsyn with his escort, rode to the rear in a Lend-Lease jeep. He was taken by rail 800 miles east to Moscow. In the Soviet capital, he was dispatched to the notorious Lubyanka Prison. Solzhenitsyn's friends tell an amusing anecdote about the prisoner's trip through Moscow from the railroad depot. It seems that his "hay-foot" police escort, made up of peasant lads who had never been to the big city, got lost en route from the station to the prison. They had to ask the prisoner, Solzhenitsyn, directions to the greenish edifice in the center of Moscow not far from the Kremlin which houses the basements where well-known Old Bolsheviks and countless alleged enemies of Stalin had been summarily executed in the late 1930s.

From Lubyanka (where he was beaten as he was being interrogated), he was dispatched to correctional camps near Moscow to begin serving the eight-year sentence handed down by a three-man "Special Tribunal" of the N.K.G.B. (People's Commissariat of Public Security), under Article 58 of the RSFSR Criminal Code. Among the projects worked upon by "Zek" (prisoner) Solzhenitsyn during these first months of hard labor was a group of multiple-apartment dwellings at Building No. 30 on Lenin Prospect in the Soviet capital. In 1946, he was sent to an M.G.B. group research institute on Moscow's outskirts - the subject of some of the material found in *The First Circle*. After four years here, he served out most of the last three years of his sentence in a new labor camp for political prisoners set up in Central Kazakhstan, to a settlement called Dzezhazgan is Karaganda Province, an area known for forced labor camps and settlements. It was in this camp in southwestern Siberia that Solzhenitsyn conceived of the idea for *One Day in the Life of Ivan Denisovich*. Zek Solzhenitsyn worked as a brick-layer and foundryman in this labor camp.

The man who inspired Solzhenitsyn's character in *One Day*, Buinovsky (modeled after B. V. Burkovsky) remembers Solzhenitsyn, his fellow prisoner, as a good friend, "honest ... taciturn ... never getting mixed up in loud discussions" (from Izvestiya, USSR, Jan. 15,1964, before the anti-Khrushchev guard was able to reorient the party line against the author of *One Day*).

It was in this camp, too, that Solzhenitsyn contracted a nearly fatal case of cancer of the stomach (quite possibly the result of an ulcerous condition brought on partly by Solzhenitsyn's intensely high-strung, "hyper" personality). In the semi-autobiographical novel, *Cancer Ward*, the leading character Kostoglotov contracts cancer and is operated on unsuccessfully-as happened to the author.

"HALF FREE"

In March of 1953, just at the time of the death of Stalin, Solzhenitsyn was released from the prison machine-shop life of Ekibastuz, the village to which he had been transferred somewhat earlier. This was, it seemed, to become his permanent place of exile. "Half-freedom," Solzhenitsyn called it. There he resumed his work as a high-school teacher, colleagues recalling how, in these years, "he would enter the classroom like a gust of wind" and would create an atmosphere "highly conductive to creative work." The subject was, of course, mathematics. Besides teaching, he again took up his pen and began the drafting of such works as *Love-Girl and the Innocent, The First Circle*, and some verses and short stories.

In August 1953 the stomach cancer recurred, and in the following year, Solzhenitsyn was permitted treatment at a Tashkent oncological clinic (the subject of *Cancer Ward*). Finally, in the spring of 1955 he returned to the Tashkent clinic and was pronounced cured. In 1955, he began to concentrate on the writing of *The First Circle*, which is considered along with *One Day* to be among his very best writings.

In February 1956, at the beginning of the 6-year de-Stalinization drive kicked off at the 20th Party Congress, Solzhenitsyn's case went up for review by the Military Section of the USSR Supreme Court, the highest court of appeal in the country. Fortunately for him, the court announced that there had been no substance to the original charges and that all further prosecution in his case, and the punishment along with it, should be stopped. Released from exile at last, Solzhenitsyn moved westward to European Russia where he settled in Vladimir District, later moving and settling in the town of Ryazan (pronounced r-ya-ZAHN) located 100 miles to the southeast of Moscow.

Because of Solzhenitsyn's modest and unassuming way of life, and because he prefers to follow an almost ascetic, Kantian habit of life (reminiscent of the character Lensky in Pushkin's Eugene Onegin), little is known of the details of his daily life until the time of his forcible banishment from the USSR in February 1974. For that matter, not too much is known of his secluded, private life since he has begun living in the West, where he has been more or less on the move engaged as he is in research in many locations (including the U.S.), as he continues his study and writing of the early 20th-century history of his country in novel-form. In Ryazan he was known to have lived in a room over a garage which he had himself constructed, much as he had used bricks as the bricklayer Zek 232 (in Russian, III-232) in the Kazakhstan labor camp at Dzezkazgan. It was here in Ryazan that he completed such works as *One Day in the Life of Ivan Denisovich, Matryona's Place, A Candle in the Wind*, and other works.

DOWN HILL

As already related in the Introduction, in 1968 Solzhenitsyn was expelled from the Ryazan writer's union; this was the time, too, when relations between himself and his wife, Natalya, reached the point of final separation. From then on, it was downhill all the way, as far as concerned the author's relations with the Brezhnev-Kosygin regime (as told above).

The series of events began which led from the Nobel Prize for Literature, the countless "zhaloby" (letters of grievance) written to Soviet authorities and literary bureaucrats, his membership in the Soviet (dissident) Human Rights Committee, a number of interviews with foreign newsmen, and to his eventual expulsion from his homeland.

Early in 1973, less than a year before his banishment, Reshetocskaya finally withdrew her refusal to grant her husband a divorce, a refusal which had strong K.G.B. backing; Solzhenitsyn thereupon married Natalya Svetlova. But he was refused permission to live with her in an apartment off Gorky Street in Moscow. At this time, too, his lease was running out on his "dacha" (summer place) outside Moscow, all of which would have made him homeless. In August he made public a letter written to the Minister of Interior (M.V.D.) demanding that he be given the right to live where he chose. He added that police surveillance and other types of pressure were becoming unbearable: "My death," he wrote, "will not make happy those people who count on death to stop all my literary activity ... My literary last will and testament would inevitably come into force and with it, the main body of my works, including those which I have refrained from having published over the years." Obviously, he was implying that public opinion throughout the world might prove too embarrassing to the powers-that-be in Moscow (the author was working on *Gulag Archipelago*).

It was at this juncture that Solzhenitsyn penned his famous nomination of his colleague, Dr. Andrei Sakharov, for the Nobel Peace Prize. In this same message (again, published in the West, e.g., Op-Ed Page of *The New York Times*) the author not only criticized the Soviet regime but took certain elements in the West to task. He indicted those in the West who ignored the violence committed by the Communists in Vietnam (e.g., at Hue) while fixing their attention on relatively less important matters such as the apartheid policy of South Africa, Watergate, and French nuclear weapons tests. The crimes of the Soviet Union, the author maintained, are "foreboding for the future of man," and must be constantly kept in view as a tangible threat to humanity.

With *Gulag Archipelago* becoming known in the West Solzhenitsyn authorized publication of the first two of the total seven parts of the novel by the Paris YMCA publisher. At this juncture the K.G.B. proffered a deal to the author by which if he delayed publishing Gulag he would be granted the permission to publish *Cancer Ward* in the USSR. Aware of the duplicity of the K.G.B. and its poor record in keeping its end of a deal, Solzhenitsyn replied that he might delay, but apparently had no intention of doing so. Then, in the winter of 1974-75, the party press opened an extremely bitter campaign against the famous author. No holds were barred. Solzhenitsyn was called a traitor, a scoundrel, an "immoral man" (!??), a man full of hatred for the Socialist Motherland which had nourished him. As he had done before with such valor, Solzhenitsyn counterattacked, his several statements never being published in the Soviet press, of course, but which are recorded in the Western press. Asserting that he was ready to take the consequences for his words, especially those written in *Gulag Archipelago*, Solzhenitsyn said: "I have fulfilled my duty to those who perished [in Leninist-Stalinist repression]; this gives me a feeling of relief and peace of mind."

SOLZHENITSYN IS DEPORTED

In February 1974, the regime evidently decided to close in on Solzhenitsyn and settle the Solzhenitsyn case once and for all. On February 8, Solzhenitsyn refused to appear at the State's Prosecutor's office when he was given a summons to do so. He refused a second the next day. On the third day, seven K.G.B. men came to Natalya's apartment, where the author was living and informed him that he was under arrest. Solzhenitsyn thereupon picked up an overnight valise, which was already packed, put on his sheepskin overcoat, which he had worn in the camps in the 1950s, and went under duress to Lefortovo prison cross-town.

At the prison the police stripped him down, interrogated him apparently without violence, and told him that he was about to be charged with treason under Article 64 of the revised RSFSR Criminal Code. Solzhenitsyn stood his ground. He informed his abductors that he would refuse to appear in any such court under the accusation; even if he was sentenced, he said he would refuse to perform any labor in whatever camp in which he would be confined. At approximately 1 p.m. on February 13, the author was informed that by order of a special decree (ukaz) of the USSR Supreme Soviet, he would have his citizenship taken away from him and be deported. Flown out of his native country he was transported in a Soviet plane to Frankfurt, West Germany. He had been assured that his wife and three children could join him, once he had settled permanently in the West. He first stayed at and then left the home of the German author Heinrich Boll, going to Norway, then returning soon after to Germany and finally to Switzerland. His wife and children did join the author in Zurich.

During all of this furor and since, Solzhenitsyn has maintained a mostly modest silence, as he lives and works in semi-seclusion. Parts three and four of Gulag appeared in the spring of 1974. Further work on the sequels to *August 1914* has gone on, the research for which has taken the author (as far as is known) to France, Britain, Canada, the United States and other Western countries. Meantime, the author has chosen to grant very few interviews. One memorable one was with CBS's Walter Cronkite, summer 1974. Also in the same year (December 12) Solzhenitsyn granted an interview in Stockholm on the occasion of the long-delayed Nobel Prize presentation ceremony. Called the "conscience of his nation" in an excellent article about him written by highly-respected Western specialist on Russian literature, George Feifer (Reader's Digest, September 1974), the bearded Alexander Solzhenitsyn not only continues to do historical research, to write, and to raise his three sons, Dmitri, Ignaty, and Yermolai, but also to lend his support to Western private agencies who are supportive of reform in his native country and to informing the Russian people of developments in the world's human rights movement. Feifer concluded his R.D. piece: "Solzhenitsyn is no saint ... Yet ... following only his own conscience, he has in a sense triumphed, single-handed, over the massive might of a modern dictatorial state."

CRITICISM OF "ONE DAY" IN THE USSR

As we mentioned in the Introduction, Solzhenitsyn's *One Day in the Life of Ivan Denisovich* first appeared in November 1962 number of the magazine *Novy Mir*. Between the pale blue cover sheets of this well-known tolstiy (Literally, fat-one, meaning a journal thick with articles), *One Day* ran 67 pages, counting a brief but courageous page-and-a-half Preface written by the editor, Alexander Tvardovsky.

In his epoch-making introduction to this equally unprecedented event in Soviet literature, Tvardovsky said:

"The real-life material which forms the basis of A. Solzhenitsyn's story is unusual for Soviet literature. It bears the reverberations of those diseased phenomena in our society which are linked to the period of the cult of [Stalin's] person, which has been exposed and condemned by the party."

The editor, a reputed close friend of Khrushchev, went on to quote the First Secretary, from his report delivered at the 22nd ("de-Stalinizing") Party Congress (October 1961). At that time Khrushchev asserted that it was the party's duty to expose any abuses of power such as existed in the past under Stalin: "We must tell the truth to the party and to the people," the First Secretary said.

This, of course, was precisely what *One Day* did, which may have been one of the reasons why Khrushchev not only personally approved its publication in *Novy Mir*, but may even have ordered that it be published. Khrushchev's motives are quite beside the point; some say that he wished to embarrass Old Stalinists in the Presidium, realizing that he himself by no means had "clean hands" when it came to the period of Stalin purges in the late 1930s (K's own abuse of power in this period in the Ukraine is a well-known story to students of Soviet history). Tvardovsky's remark that Solzhenitsyn's story was unusual (neobyche) in Soviet literature immediately brings to mind the official Soviet literary doctrine of "socialist realism."

DOCTRINE OF SOCIALIST REALISM

The fact is that socialist **realism** did not permit the kind of frank **realism** found in *One Day*. This is what the *Novy Mir* editor meant by "unusual". According to the ideology of Marxism-Leninism-Stalinism, socialist **realism** reveals the "historical truth" of the past or present time as tailored into a novel, play, motion picture, etc., by a Soviet writer. As initially presented at the First Congress of Soviet Writers in 1934, literature was to serve the party by making "historically concrete portrayals of reality as it develops in a revolutionary way." The "truth" of an artist, the doctrine states, consists in his ability, indeed willingness, to grasp those "progressive" elements and factors in society which illustrate the "inevitable march of history" toward "revolutionary goals as defined by the party."

Soon after its promulgation, and as all sorts of "Five year Plan literature" began to roll off the presses of the state publishing houses, serious jokes about socialist **realism** began to make the rounds. The gist of these "anekdoty" was that Stalinist literature was neither "socialist" nor "realistic." Instead of the truth about "concrete reality," one joke went, came only the truth about ... concrete (the title of a well-known Five-year Plan novel about construction). "Truth" became whatever the party considered to be "progressive" at the time. The result was that a gray-shaded dullness came into Soviet art-meaning by "art" (iskusstvo) - cinema, fiction, plays painting, poetry, architecture and even music, although the latter was perhaps the least governable by the dictates of socialist realism.

After Stalin died in 1953, one of the first onslaughts against party dictation over the arts (by K. Pomerantsev - see Weeks, *Andrei Sakharov And The Soviet Dissidents*, Monarch Notes, 1975, pp. 4-8) brought up the subject of the distorted dogma of socialist **realism**. In the mid-1960s Andrei Sinyavsky, writing under the pen name Abram Terzt, crafted a brilliant satirical Essay entitled What Is Socialist **Realism**? (it appeared only on the samizdat circuit, of course). Among other things, Sinyavsky-Tertz complained that socialist **realism** permits only lacquered heroes; there is no place, as there is in foreign literature for "lost illusions broken hope unfulfilled dreams ... which are contrary to socialist realism." In Soviet literature, the author continued, the hero or heroine dies at the end, but "Communism triumphs."

With the cult of socialist **realism** as a tradition in Soviet literature and the official promulgation of it by an arts bureaucracy represented by the tradition of Zhdanovsh china (from A. A. Zhdanov, post World War II party secretary and interpreter of party dogmas in the arts), one can well imagine the shock which greeted *One Day in the Life of Ivan Denisovich*. But once the shock had subsided, any number of officially-approved critics began to weigh in heavily on the side of *One Day*.

Even the customarily hard-line critic, A. Dymshits, greeted the work with enthusiastic praise. Another critic in *Izvestiya* described Solzhenitsyn as a "true helper of the party in a sacred and vital cause - the struggle against the cult of personality and its consequences." V. Yermilov, writing in *Pravda*, described the author of *One Day* as "gifted with a rare talent [who] has told us a truth which cannot be forgotten, that must not be forgotten. [His story] calls to mind Tolstoy's artistic power in its depiction of the national character." Any number of other critics voiced their support for *One Day* and its author- in Literaturnaya Gazeta, Literaturnaya Rossiya, and in any number of journals or statements by Soviet literary figures. All this was permitted, perhaps encouraged, before the anti-Khrushchev, pro-Stalin-rehabilitation group began closing in on the First Secretary and the de-Stalinization program. Once this reactionary counterattack was underway, eventually leading to the overthrow of the First Secretary himself, critics like Lydia Fomenko in Literaturnaya Rossiya began to appraise *One Day* and Solzhenitsyn quite differently. For example, N. Seliverstov wrote in Literaturnaya Gazeta (October 1963) that Solzhenitsyn's story was unrealistic since it was written about events "in life as it existed the day before yesterday" (an **allusion** to the one-day picture portrayed by Solzhenitsyn). Genuine justice, he went on, was "won by the party... [it] runs through our life today and is triumphant!"

As late as January 1964, a famous pro-*One Day* piece appeared, not surprisingly in *Novy Mir*. This was the memorable article by Vladimir I. Lakshin, deputy editor to Tvardovsky. Lakshin is (or was) a highly-respected authority on Russian literature, with a record for satirical, if Aesopian, attacks against hack, cliche-ridden Soviet writing. Part of his article, which he titled "Friends and Foes of Ivan Denisovich," was devoted to striking back at the many critics who had attacked *One Day* and its author over the preceding months. Another part of his piece concerned the cardinal virtues of *One Day*. This novella, he wrote, "excludes empty sensationalism [and] the desire to shock with descriptions and suffering and physical pain." Instead, said Lakshin, the author had a larger task. "Were Solzhenitsyn an artist of smaller stature and less sensitivity, he would probably have selected the worst day in the most arduous period of Ivan Denisovich's camp life. But he took a different path ... [thereby] ensuring the full objectivity of his artistic testimony, and all the more mercilessly and sharply struck a blow at the crimes of the recent past."

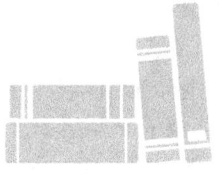

ONE DAY IN THE LIFE OF IVAN DENISOVICH

....

"Solzhenitsyn is the heir, not only of the best tendencies in early socialist **realism**, but also of the great literary tradition, and above all that of Tolstoy and Dostoyevsky," wrote Georg Lukacs, the octogenarian Marxist literary critic of Communist Hungary. In mentioning Dostoyevsky in the same breath with Solzhenitsyn and *One Day*, Lukacs is of course mindful of the fact that Dostoyevsky, too, wrote a book about life under the conditions of Siberian exile (House of the Dead, 1862). He may also have remembered that House of the Dead was exactly 100 years old when its Soviet successor, *One Day*, burst into print. Unlike Dostoyevsky's book, however, *One Day* is not full of the horrors of camp life, nor does it indulge in the kind of polemics one finds in the vehement condemnation of Siberian exile in Dostoyevsky's novel. There are other differences, too. Dostoyevsky employed the first person; Solzhenitsyn for the most part does not. Dostoyevsky's prisoners, for all the extreme conditions of the Tsarist penal colonies, fare somewhat better than their counterparts under the Lenin-Stalin camps-Tsarist prisoners, at least had adequate food, clothing, and spare time. (One is reminded of Lenin's own relatively short sojourn in Siberian exile and how this intelligentka was able to fish, swim, ski, write revolutionary articles, and send and receive uncensored mail!) Finally, the prisoners of 100 years ago always had the thought in the back of their minds that someday they would be freed; Ivan Shukhov and his friends, the characters of Solzhenitsyn's *One Day*, often viewed their terms as endless; "they are bored with counting" the remaining years in their stretches.

Although Lukacs compares Solzhenitsyn to Tolstoy, we have already noted how different were their two perspectives on the past, on history. Their methods of telling a story are quite different, too. In true nineteenth-century style, Tolstoy builds long descriptions of his characters (not unlike the technique employed by Dickens), as he places them in a multitude of situations and episodes, often analyzing their reactions in minute detail. Solzhenitsyn on the other hand brushes in his characterizations with the light touch of a watercolorist. Moreover, in the supercooled treatment of Shukhov, for example, the emotional coloring becomes the pale blue of a mild-winter Siberian sky while characters' mental reactions to this or that privation or inhumane act in the labor camp seems to be as neutral-white as snow.

One Western critic sees a resemblance in style between Solzhenitsyn and Anton Chekhov, the great Russian playwright. Chekhov, of course, is famous for understatement and sparseness of emotion, although the situation (as in the mother-son confrontation in Sea Gull) may be potentially supercharged with emotional tension. For the audience, it's "all the same," as Chekhov's characters are wont to utter - in that, the emotional charge is all the greater for having been understated. Perhaps the key word for Solzhenitsyn's and Chekhov's approaches to life is "laconism": i.e., a semblance of taciturnity, of conciseness and economy, both of mood and expression. In *The First Circle*, the main character Nerzhin makes a remark which illustrates the laconic streak in Solzhenitsyn: "Descriptions of prison life tend to overdo the horror of it. Surely it is more frightening when there is no actual (nastoyashchiy) terror; what is truly terrifying is the changeless routine which followed year after year." Solzhenitsyn could even speak ironically of the *Gulag Archipelago*, in the Preface to the work of the same name, as "that monstrous world that I have come almost to love," it is not "something shameful [or] a nightmare."

The very opening of *One Day in the Life of Ivan Denisovich* sets the tone for the whole story. "V pyat' chasov utra, kak vsegda…" "At five o'clock in the morning, like always…" In this way, the author indicates that what he is about to relate will be nothing out of the ordinary. The prisoner Ivan Shukhov is waking up on a usual, cold, camp day - or, as we learn, on a day which turned out to be not quite as cold as other days ("it was nowhere near - 41C."); at the very end of the story, we learn that this one day was "without a dark cloud; almost a happy day." But we would not likely gather that it was so "happy," except in a sardonic sense.

CINEMATIC QUALITY

Solzhenitsyn continues opening his story with straightforward, unemotional descriptions of Shukhov's surroundings. Ice two-fingers-thick on the window panes. The nameless campguard sounding reveille by clanging on a piece of track rail with a huge hammer. The pitch darkness of the early morning with only a dim, yellow glow cast on the frozen window pane by three electric lights, "two in the outer area, one inside the camp itself." No wonder that the screenwriter and producers of the film version could see the movie possibilities of such descriptions, from the very opening words of Ivan Denisovich. In the movie scenario, the opening of Scene 1 was scripted as follows:

"Fade In

"1 Ext. The Camp-High Angle (Helicopter Shot) - Before Dawn

From a distance the camp looks like a solitary star in the cosmos: it glows a sickly yellow; its circles of light are no more than a luminous blur. Beyond the star, as far as the eye can see, is snow.

"It seems like the middle of the night.

"It is intensely cold.

"The Camera Moves In Very Slowly

Superimpose Main Titles And Titles

Gradually it becomes possible to distinguish more of the area of the camp: two powerful searchlights sweeping from watchtowers on the outer perimeter; a circle of border lights marks the barbed wire fences; the shapes of the huts and other buildings become discernible; the gates, the near watchtowers with their guards and machine guns, the prison block, the mess hall, the staff quarters.

"End Credits And Titles...

"Cut To

"2 Int. Hut 9 - Before Dawn

"Under a blanket and a coat lies Ivan Denisovich..."

Incidentally, the film, jointly produced by Group W Films, Norsk Films, and Leontes Productions in 1970, was shot under the most adverse and realistic of conditions. Sub-zero temperatures in the Norwegian village of Roros had the actors Tom Courtenay (Ivan Shukhov), Espen Skjonberg (Tiurin), et al., in a state of almost perpetual shivers. This prompted Courtenay to remark at the end of the 11 weeks of shooting, "I feared the worst, but when I got there [to the Norwegian location], I enjoyed the cold, I enjoyed fighting it. It was ... a single-minded and pure atmosphere." Solzhenitsyn saw and liked the picture. He called it "good [and] honest," although it lacked "Russian local color."

Needless to say, the main character of *One Day* is Ivan Denisovich Shukhov. He is the first character to appear in the story and his presence is constantly with us throughout the whole. Moreover, Solzhenitsyn makes use of his main character in a number of ways. First, we view much of the physical and spiritual life of the Siberian "special camp" for political prisoners through Ivan Denisovich's eyes-sometimes as dialogue and sometimes as a third-person observer; at times an invisible narrator describes situations in which the main character is not placed or in which he could not be present in any case.

SELF-RESPECTING CHARACTERS

Second, in Ivan Denisovich, Solzhenitsyn has hewn a sharply-angled character whose economy of speech is as lean as his body, whose mind is as crystal clear as the icicles which form from the sweat dripping from his brow. But he is not a grim man facing his last three years of camp confinement with bitterness and humorlessness. On the contrary, Shukhov has at once an animal-like determination to survive and a human-like compulsion even to prosper (as well as can be under the circumstances). Shukhov never succumbs to corruption or to any serious immorality whatsoever; he and most of the other dozen main characters in the story maintain their self-respect, and do so with quiet, unassuming pride.

Third, by focusing principally on one character, the author is able to "dissect" his personality, his reactions to the various demands placed upon him, and to present in microcosm, like a miniaturized Russian Easter egg, the millions of other prisoners who endured similar or probably worse fates in the hundreds of other labor camps under Lenin and Stalin, and their successors. As the scenario of the film version reads, "The camp looks like a solitary star in the cosmos." So does Ivan Denisovich. But in concentrating on Shukhov, Solzhenitsyn does not isolate him from the others. Instead, we compare and contrast other prisoners' reactions to the same ordeals, or opportunities, with Shukhov's. Take for example, the somewhat fanatic Baptist prisoner, Alyosha, whose name is a bit of double entendre on the author's part for we are, and at the same time we are not, reminded of the "religious brother," Alyosha of the three Brothers Karamazov. Alyosha (or Alyoshka) reads his Bible aloud, tries to convert his colleagues, including Shukhov, to his form of religion, but turns off Ivan Denisovich with his (Alyosha's) excessive concern, it seems to Ivan, with heaven and hell rather than with the moral character of Jesus. At one point, Alyosha intones, "'Give us this day our daily bread'!" Whereupon Shukhov remarks, "Our bread ration, don't you mean?"

In the minute analysis of Shukhov, we get the picture of a largely stoic, almost submissive but definitely not "resigned" individual who has served out 7 of his 10 years at the camp for criminal-types (non-political) at Ust-Izhma in the north and is now down the home stretch at the second, somewhat less severe camp for "politicals." Although he is surrounded by various forms of inhumanity and degradation (mainly on the part of camp officials and their toadies among the prisoners), Shukhov and his comrades do not submit to any of the sundry temptations. Instead of "gold-bricking," they take pride in the various work assignments that they perform. This is especially true of Ivan Denisovich; moreover, his diligence is not artificial. It rather comes natural to him. In his various imperfections, which tend to be minor and "expected" under the circumstances, the main character becomes completely credible and sympathetic without being mawkishly so.

SOLZHENITSYN AND THE CLASSICAL TRINITY.

One of the most insightful discussions of Solzhenitsyn's main character may be found in Lopukhina-Rodzyanko's *The Spiritual Roots of Solzhenitsyn's Writings* (published by Possev-Verlag, Frankfurt/Main, in Russian). Lopukhina-Rodzyanko finds a heightened spiritual, even religious, consciousness in most of the author's works and in *One Day* in particular. Not only, she writes, is Solzhenitsyn committed to the classical trinity of Beauty, Truth, and Justice, he links the personal conscience of each of his heroes to universal human justice and social consciousness. In the personal lives of his heroes-Ivan Denisovich's, for example - the character ekes out a spiritually satisfying existence no matter how trying the circumstances because of the character's "harmoniously structured psyche." Ivan Denisovich's psyche possesses this inner harmony, since in an almost "geological sense" Shukhov is an archetypical peasant-representative of Mother Russia; Shukhov's moral fiber is from the people and is spontaneous. Somewhat passive though he may be, Ivan is not meek like Alyosha and is not prepared to make a surrender as

Alyosha is; he will not be overcome. The critic also finds in Ivan Denisovich Shukhov an elemental comradeliness, a desire to come to the assistance of his fellow zeks. Ivan tends to regard his work team as a "second family." For it, he is prepared to cross mountains or take any risk. Ivan's human traits and basically sympathetic nature reveal itself at the end of the day when he sees the brigade leader, Fetiukov, downtrodden and weeping. "Shukhov pities Fetiukov because the brigade leader lacks a satisfactory approach to life, which is so clear and natural to Shukhov," Lopukhina-Rodzyanko writes.

MEANING OF NAMES

On the matter of the character's name, Lopukhina-Rodzyanko, sharing the view of some other critics, believes that the names Ivan and Alyosha were deliberately invented by Solzhenitsyn to suggest a parallel with the characters of the same first names in The Brothers Karamazov. Ivan Karamazov also denies the existence or even the use of heaven and hell, unlike Alyosha Karamazov who defends their existence and necessity. Both Ivans love life and people, both wish to lighten the burden of existence on earth, as, theoretically, so also did the Grand Inquisitor. Still, Solzhenitsyn separates love of man from love of abstract justice; both his and Dostoyevsky's Alyoshas place the latter higher than the former. Solzhenitsyn himself remarked on this point in his "Answer to Three Students": "Love of justice seems to me to be different from love for one's fellow man (or, at least, is only partially equivalent to it)." Thus, Alyosha the Baptist (in *One Day*) may seem to be a character who is spiritually superior to the hero, Ivan Denisovich. "Alyosha the Baptist," writes Lopukhina-Rodzyanko, "is the most striking symbol of the righteous man in all the writings of Solzhenitsyn."

BIBLICAL PARALLELS

Finally, the critic notes the striking parallel between the "temptations" confronting Ivan Denisovich in the camp and the temptations of Christ described by Matthew in the Gospels, 4:1-10. For forty days and forty nights, Christ was tempted by the Devil in the desert. In the first temptation, the Devil challenges Jesus to convert stones into bread. To which Jesus replies: "Man shall not live by bread alone." In the second temptation, the Devil takes Christ to the holy city and places Him "on the pinnacle of the temple and saith unto Him, If thou art the Son of God, cast thyself down ... Jesus said unto him ... Thou shalt not make trial of the Lord thy God." In the third temptation, the Devil takes him up a high mountain and shows Jesus "all the kingdoms of the world, and the glory.... All these things I will give thee if thou wilt fall down and worship me." Jesus answers the Devil: "Thou shalt worship the Lord thy God, and Him only shalt thou serve."

The analogy to the first Biblical temptation in *One Day* is the not-by-bread-alone quality of life in the camp.

At one point in the story, Shukhov remarks that you have to eat "with all your mind on the food," not like in the past before confinement when this distortion of values did not exist. In another part, Shukhov notes "your life is ruled by a couple of ounces of bread."

As to the second temptation, Solzhenitsyn teaches that man's survival (in camp or anywhere else) cannot depend on miracles or challenges put to the Lord, as it were. In *One Day*, this is seen in the notion that sick-call, or the reliance on the infirmary in order to survive, is not only an easy way out of the ordeal of living and working in the "white desert," or in

Siberian exile, it is no solution at all. It is merely a weak-willed, temporary, "miraculous" solution for overcoming difficulties. Ivan Denisovich feels shamefaced about going on sick-call on that morning unless he is really very ill. The narrator notes, as Ivan sits in the infirmary awaiting the orderly, Kolya: "The infirmary seemed alien to him." In the end, he is relieved to find out that he is not sick, that his temperature is under 100 degrees. At the end of the story, proudly he remarks that he has gotten through this one day without being sick. Sickness - the "miracle," in this case-was avoided; man will survive on his own terms, without miraculous intervention. The infirmary represents a renunciation of man's will, his dependence on a miracle. Man has his fate in his own hands, says Solzhenitsyn, whether this concerns his health or the preservation of his conscience.

The parallelism with the third Biblical temptation relates to the zeks' refusal to bow down to any Satans among them- when they have the choice, as they do when their wills are free to express themselves, as in fighting hunger and cold. Only when they are not in a position to exert their wills, to assert their humanity, are they subject to the commands of the Devil, as represented by the camp authorities and the System. Anyone in *One Day* who swindles his way through his stretch and who greases his palms or plays "King Rat" (from James Clavell's novel) is scorned as a person who submits to Satan. Kolya, who works in a warm, "cushy" job in the infirmary - the "sharashka" arrangement (technicians in a special prison or section of a prison) - has sold his soul to the Devil.

OTHER CHARACTERS AND MAIN EPISODES

The slivers of life strung together in *One Day* suggest the film-strip quality of the daily life of any individual. In a single day, there are little stings, little happinesses, little letdowns, etc., but these rivulets seem to flow in and out of the larger stream of our very natures, of our whole lives. As in any individual's day, there are a number of brief encounters, or "knots" of action. In such encounters, we reveal ourselves to others just as others reveal themselves to us.

Within the matrix of such **episodes** in *One Day*, the moods characters, and the narrative follow their various serpentine trails; at the same time, the undercurrent of Solzhenitsyn's special philosophy of life engulfs all these partialities.

SOLZHENITSYN'S IRONY

Take the thermometer **episode** early on in the story. Several squad leaders, on their way to the Planning and Production Division (P.P.D.), gather near a pole upon which a large thermometer is affixed. One of the younger men, a former Hero of the Soviet Union, shinnies up the pole and wipes off the gauge.

"Don't breathe on it," someone shouts, "or it'll go up."

"Go up? Fucking likely that would happen. I won't change it!" Then he reads the temperature which is a "modest" - 27.5 C. Someone observes: "It's never right. It always lies... But then, why hang up an accurate one, anyway?"

The "it-always-lies" remark, the **irony** of a Hero of the Soviet Union doing the job of reading the thermometer, is the author's way of showing that even that most important matter to the prisoners - the degree of "frost" on any given day which determines whether and what kind of work will be performed on that day - is the subject of "lying." (One is here reminded of a short writing - and appeal - by Solzhenitsyn entitled, Live Not According to a Lie.) Also, as Solzhenitsyn frequently shows, the general mass of the prisoners sometimes display an anarchic, don't-give-a-damn attitude toward the camp and their life in it. This makes a striking contrast to the high seriousness with which Ivan Denisovich and his group of some dozen prisoners for the most part regard their life and the preservation of their humanity and of principle. It seems scarcely likely that the more upstanding of characters, such as KILGAS for example, would ever relish the fact of the thermometer's being inaccurate. "Why hang up an accurate one, anyway" would probably not be uttered by the more conscientious types among Ivan's colleagues.

In an encounter, also early in the book, between a guard and Ivan, Ivan has unintentionally splashed some water on the guard's boots (valenki).

"Hey there, scum, watch what you're doing!" Ivan thereupon must clean the guard's soiled boot. Apparently, he accidentally uses too much water as he tries to clean it and the guard exclaims, "Hey, idiot! How much water are you going to use!"

"I'll never get it clean otherwise, Citizen Chief. It's thick with mud," Ivan replies.

"Didn't you ever observe your wife scrubbing the floor, you swine!" Whereupon Ivan remarks ingenuously-neither out of malice nor self-pity: "I was taken from my wife in '41, Citizen Chief. I've quite forgotten just what she was like." The guard then observes, quite out of "synch" with what Ivan has just said: "That's the way the scum wash.... They don't know how to do a fucking thing and they don't want to learn, either. They're not worth the bread (khleb) we give them. What we ought to do is feed them shit."

In this encounter, or "knot," the author shows us the essentially stolid insensitivity of the guard element in the camp. Since he frequently shows lines of continuity running between life inside and life outside the camp in normal Soviet society, this **episode** illustrates, as many others do, the brutishness of a "Citizen Chief." There are many "Citizen Chiefs" on the other side of the barbed wire, too. Another use of this **episode** is to show that the guard is so uncaring that he does not realize that Ivan Denisovich is someone who does know how to do something, as we see as the story progresses. In fact, the narrator (the author concealed) asserts soon after this scene, "Shukhov knew how to cope with anything." As he is washing the floor in this same scene, the observation is made that "work is like a stick. It has two ends. When you work for those who know the difference, you give them a quality performance. But for the fools, you put on a show (pokazukhu)."

In the mess hall scene-at the first meal of the day on that one day-it is a "rare occasion" since Ivan can go right in without the usual long wait (again: the "one day" is not so bad, as days go!). This situation affords the author the opportunity to observe the incarcerated men, with so little to lose, engaged in the potentially civilized business of feeding themselves. Are they pigs? Or do they comport themselves almost like gentlemen? How do they relate to each other at such a delicate time, when it might well be "every man for himself"?

The first thing we learn is that the food is meager and miserable. The men are obliged to get along with bits of fish and cabbage leaves. Some breakfast! But "to spit the bones on the floor was considered somehow to be bad manners." We are introduced here to FETIUKOV; he is the man who holds Shukhov's meal for him since Shukhov was delayed by a side trip to the guard house, where he thought he was going to be penalized for having arisen a bit late at reveille; as it was, he got off free, thanks to a nameless Tartar guard. Fetiukov is described as low man on the totem pole, as far as the other members of Shukhov's barracks team are concerned; a man you give little jobs to, like watching after your plate if you were late, he is also described as a "jackal."

Next, Shukhov removes from his boot that all-important implement which he never overlooks and which he looks after with such care: his spoon. The spoon had been with him at the northern camp, too, and he had made it-cast it-himself. Taking his hat off (another gesture to civilization, but one which Ivan Denisovich takes most seriously), he starts in on the cold gruel. The author notes wrily that the gruel had not been poured either from the top or from the bottom of the boiling pot. A medium serving, in other words, not unlike the day as a whole - not good, not bad. "Fetiukov wouldn't be above filching a spud as he guarded [Ivan's] bowl." Ivan likes the gruel mainly because it is hot. And he eats it with his usual deliberateness - "no need to rush-even if the roof caught on fire." Minutes count under such circumstances: "Not counting sleeping hours, a prisoner lived for himself for only 10 minutes in the morning at breakfast, 5 minutes at lunch, and 5 more at suppertime."

Observations are made by the unseen narrator about the condition of the food at various times of the year. June is the best year-groats instead of tasteless vegetables. July was the worst time-shredded nettles boiled in water.

PITY FOR A FISH?

As he proceeds to extract every morsel of fish from the almost skeletal mass lying in his bowl, his every action is described by the narrator. Tail, fins, gills, head-all chewed and swallowed. As for the eyes, Ivan, we're told, treats them with a certain respect, much to the amusement of the other prisoners, who tease him for it. If the fish eyes are in the head, they get eaten along with the head, but if they are floating in the liquid mass of bones and flesh, Ivan leaves them be. Solzhenitsyn makes no comment on this and we are left wondering why Shukhov would do this. Is it perhaps, out of a faint sense of pity-even for a mere fish?

After the gruel and fish comes the porridge made of magara, a "Chinese" oatmeal. This is served to him in a frozen block which must be broken into little pieces, like chopping ice. Quite tasteless, it is actually a kind of grass.

The next scene is also illustrative of life in the labor camp as well as Soviet life in general.

REVEALING INFIRMARY EPISODE

Shukhov had arisen that morning feeling ill. Because of this he had awakened late. This is an offense, so his first trip had been to the guard house, where he had been let off, thanks to the Tartar. Then he had gone for breakfast. He had almost decided not to go to the infirmary while he was mopping the floor in the guard house (where the spilling accident had taken place) - the work made him feel better, at least for the moment. But after the meal, he thought he would have to go after all. (Note here that Ivan Denisovich is not "exploiting" sick call; also that the brief spell of work he did on his hands and knees made him feel somewhat better.) He even passed up a "connection" between himself and the Tall Latvian whose packages sent from outside sometimes contained fragrant tobacco for rolling into cigarettes. The infirmary **episode** is one of the most revealing of the story. Nor was it overlooked by the scenarist, Ronald Harwood, in doing the movie version of *One Day*.

Upon entering the infirmary, Ivan finds that nobody is about: "The doctors can't be out of bed yet." But Kolya (short for Nikolai) Vdovushkin, a "medical assistant," is sitting behind a "clean little table and is dressed in a sparkling white coat." He is writing and Shukhov notices that whatever it is he is writing, it is not infirmary or camp business-probably "something private and none of [Ivan's] business." Ivan says, somewhat shamefacedly, "Listen, Nikolai Semyonich, I'm feeling ... sort of ... under the weather."

"Why are you so late?" comes the abrupt remark from the orderly. He treats Shukhov coarsely, although he knows that Ivan Denisovich does not often go on sick call, is no hypochondriac or sick-bay lounger. Kolya shoves a thermometer into him, grudgingly (the infirmary has already used up its quota of two morning sick-callees), as he comments that Shukhov has come to the infirmary just before assembly and body count. While his temperature is being taken, Shukhov has a few more precious minutes to himself. He notes that the number, 111-584, is fading from his jacket. - "It better be repainted if he wants to keep out of trouble." He feels the growth of a beard on his face - "Quiet a stubble since his last bath more than 10 days ago." That would be remedied in just three days when bath time rolled around again. "Why wait in a long barber's line? There was no one to beautify himself for."

Shukhov also muses about the Doctor, Stepan Grigorich. He was a loud-mouthed individual, contemptuous of patients, a man who had never himself known any physical labor ("If he had spent a little time laying block, then he would keep his mouth shut, you can be sure."). Moreover, the doctor's notion of convalescence was for patients to do heavy manual labor. The narrator observes: "He should have understood that even a horse can die of overwork."

Shukhov turns again to observe Kolya. Ah! He's writing poetry. Well, after all, he is a former literature major, not a medical student, a young man whom the doctor found quite useful to perform various tasks for him-quite illegitimately, since the young man was giving "ignorant" prisoners intravenous injections. "Medical Assistant" was only a label pinned on him by the doctor. Moreover, it seems the doctor rather relished his assistant's poetry; he could write verses in prison which he "had not been able to write as a free man." The assistant, it seems, had once been arrested, apparently in college, but for what we are not told.

Like everything else about the one day, Shukhov's temperature was neither high nor low but rather indifferent. It was under 99 degrees; it had to register 100 degrees to call the patient "sick." "I can't keep you here as a sick one," Kolya asserts, "but if you want to stay at your own risk..." He informs Shukhov that if the doctor pronounces him ill, O.K.; but if it turns out he is not ill, "It'll be the cells [solitary] for you." Finally, Kolya advises Ivan to go on to work. Shukhov receives the advice in total silence, makes no gesture, pulls the cap over his eyes, and exits. The narrator comments: "There's no point in expecting someone who's warm to understand someone who's cold."

SOLZHENITSYN ON SOVIET MEDICINE

These observations of one day at a prison infirmary recall some observations made by the author 12 years later when he could speak freely to a group of foreign newsmen in Stockholm when the belated award of the Nobel Prize was bestowed on him. At the press conference, December 12, 1974, Solzhenitsyn said of socialized medicine as practiced and administered in the USSR:

"Of course, we do have ... so-called free medical treatment, but [it] is all so officious, neglected, and of such low quality because employees are badly paid. The national health is certainly free of charge and open to all. But it is so organized that, starting with the Kremlin, every organization, all the minor regional and local party leaders, try to corner their own section of the medical service so as to get special treatment. And any person who has the chance to get private treatment tries to do so because the public sector will only provide him with the very poorest service. It is not because the doctors are not good, but because there is a lack of decent conditions. They have to treat 9 patients per hour-sometimes including minor operations and serious examinations. But all this must be viewed as being part of the System ... the System is directed against human beings. It is directed so as to cut off in man all that is finest and most noble in humanity."

The absent doctor, the rigid rules about numbers of sick-callees, the doctor's hard-labor therapy theory, etc., not only tell something about a labor-camp infirmary, but suggest some of the inhumanity remarked about by Solzhenitsyn as he described the medical service in normal Soviet society. As the Marxist critic, Georg Lukacs, has observed: "[Solzhenitsyn] has made his skillful grey monochrome of camp life into a symbol of everyday life under Stalin." Another critic added, "... and after [Stalin]" (Christopher Moody).

When he returns "home" to Hut 9, where his work squad, 104, lives, there is some business with his bread ration, the Baptist Alyosha, and the narrator's observations about camp life.

The second-in-command, the Ukrainian Pavlo, gives Ivan Denisovich his (allegedly) 550 g. of bread topped with a small pile of sugar. Accustomed to the inattentive way the bread is doled out to camp prisoners (Shukhov, after all, has been "sitting" for 7 years before now), Ivan estimates the true weight of his ration. Since prisoners are not permitted watches, even shirt pockets, let alone scales, they have no way of measuring anything. "It's about 20 g. short," Shukhov estimates. He wants to put part of it away to munch later but past experience teaches that orderlies have been known to find and steal prisoners' rations. So Ivan takes up needle and thread and begins sewing - stezh, stezh, stezh-stitch-stitch-stitch - the morsel of bread into his hand-packed sawdust mattress. While he is stitching furiously-there is no time to lose, assembly is in any minute- Alyosha is "evangelizing" (agitirovat') in the lower bunk. The narrator observes that Alyosha is a "crafty one" who one knew how to conceal his little Bible by making a perfectly camouflaged hole in the wall that escapes the attention of guards at every inspection.

After the sewing, Ivan's bed-making activity is described along with the elaborate preparations necessary in order to dress warmly for the day's outdoor work. You wrapped your feet with cloths, the good ones nearest your feet allowed by the torn ones for the outside. Over these rags you slipped on your boots.

The next segment is the assembling in formation to march off to work. Everyone in 104 hoped that the day's work would not carry them to the dreaded Socialist Way of Life settlement, which is as barren as the surface of the moon and just about as cold moon is in shadow). But instead of the Sotsbytgorodok (or a shorter acronym for the Socialist Way of Life settlement, Sotsgorodok) the men are told at the last minute that their work will be performed at the power-station construction site. This, like the day as a whole, is not good but not bad either. In any case, at this site the men will toil in sub-zero weather, with knife-like winds, no shelter, no really warm fires.

First, roll call. Pantaleyev is missing. "That son-of-a-bitch, staying behind again. No, he wasn't ill, the security boys were keeping him back. Squealing on someone." It was a frequent event, the camp M.G.B. holding Pantaleyev for questioning; he was the unit's stool-pigeon. In order to make the detention look regular, the M.G.B. would "fix it all up with the medical authorities" (another **allusion** to abuse of the medical service).

During roll call comes the painting on of new numbers. This is done by three camp artists who, among other things, paint nice little pictures for the camp administration. Solzhenitsyn compares the painting of numbers on prisoners' caps "like a priest anointing your brow." Shukhov gets touched up by an old-man "artist" whose hand was so stiff with cold, he could hardly manage the curly-cues of the numbers 8...5...4. (Incidentally, the Russian letter W preceding the number 854 is the 26th letter in the alphabet which translates into 26,000 to which is added 854, together indicating that Shukhov was the 26,854th prisoner added into the given camp complex. Solzhenitsyn's real number when he himself was a prisoner was W-232.)

As the men are standing for roll call, Lieutenant Volkovoi, the security chief, appears. The order is given to strip to the waist-in the sub-zero weather. Just why this unusual procedure is required this day, the men do not know. But Volkovoi lives up to his name (it comes from the Russian word for wolf). Solzhenitsyn describes him in such a way that there is little doubt that this security man resembles the Soviet Union's "first security chief," back in Lenin's day, the head of the Cheka, Felix Dzerzhinski. Like

Dzerzhinski, Volkovoi is dark, tall, with a scowl on his face, and quick in his movements. Volkovoi used to carry a whip of plaited leather which he would lay on the back of a prisoner's neck, if he felt like it, lashing him and exclaiming. "Why aren't you standing in line?" Victims of such lashings wiped away the blood but held their tongues lest they be consigned to the solitary cells.

During the frisking, we are given an insight into another character in Shukhov's work team 104, Buinovsky. Buinovsky had been a Navy commander who, as Solzhenitsyn remarks, "could not get his ship out of his system."! Buinovsky could be concealing a "cummerbund or something"! As for Shukhov, "There is nothing but my soul in my chest." No civvies underneath, no mail, no knife, no hidden food, etc., etc. Buinovsky becomes enraged at the heartless way the men are asked to strip to the waist. "You've no right to strip men in the cold," he complains. "You do not know Article 9 of the Criminal Code.... You're not behaving like Soviet people...like Communists." (Reading this in *Novy Mir* in 1962 must have been quite a shock. Soviet journal-readers were not used to such frankness; Solzhenitsyn and *Novy Mir* Editor Tvardovsky took the risk of educating their readers in candor.)

As the roll call and the frisking end, Solzhenitsyn observes: "A man is worth more than gold" (a play on Stalin's famous aphorism that human capital is worth more than money capital). Meanwhile, the guard dog "bared its fangs as if it were laughing at the zeks."

Once on their way to the power-station construction site, the column of prisoners, their hands clasped behind them, their heads lowered to avoid the stinging winds, moved along top-top, skrip-skrip (Russian for the sound made by boots in the snow) "as though at a funeral." Each zek was plunged into deep thought; unlike on warm days when each would converse with his neighbor in line. Shukhov, too, began thinking of home. Letters from his wife disturbed him. Things were changing back in the village. Now people worked in the village while also "working on the side." Meaning by that, they went into the cities to work in factories or peat-processing plants. "The kolkhoz was kept going by the women who'd been there since 1930," half the men not returning from the war. "That men were not working in their own village - this really bothered him. Only migrant workers, eh? Traveling around? But how could the village cope with the haymaking?" Other kolkhozniks, his wife had written him, had taken up carpet-painting to earn a few extra kopecks and rubles. Carpet-painters did pretty well; some had sent their offspring to a technical school. Shukhov then fantasizes about how these carpets look: "The 'Troika,' an officer in the hussars driving a splendid troika; the 'Reindeer'; and a third of Persian design.... Since a real carpet cost not fifty but thousands of rubles, people all over the country snatched these out of the painters' hands." (An average kolkhoznik's monthly wage-in kind plus small cash-amounted then to about 30-50 rubles.) Finally, as he daydreams, Shukhov decides that he won't become a carpet-maker on the side when (and if) he returns "truly home" (the barracks is never really home, even semantically): "Easy money weighs light in the hand and doesn't give you the feeling that you have really earned it. The old proverb is true: 'What you don't pay for, you don't get value for, either.' He still had a strong pair of hands. Surely, when he was out, he would find respectable work-as a plumber, a carpenter, a repairman."

CAMP AS MICROCOSM OF THE NATION

We get a closer look at Tiurin. He is the squad leader toward whom you had better be respectful. But he's not such a bad sort;

in any case, there are those who stand much higher than he, and he can be counted on to defend the squad's (likewise, his own) interests on occasion. Moreover, Tiurin had picked Shukhov to be on his team. He enjoys certain benefits, as squad leader, but he is no "King Rat." Another prisoner, this one a become-foreman named DER, pronounced "dare," derived from Russian der'mo (excrement), makes his appearance at this point in the story as the column moves toward the work site. He is frankly described as "swine" and is a civilian attached to the camp. Later in the story, the narrator, who is thinking Shukhov's thoughts, notes that Der thinks of himself as some sort of "engineer," but whenever he has lent advice to the working zeks, the advice has been useless (this suggests the common custom of Soviet party leaders, in the locales or from the Kremlin, to go "out in the fields" or to the "work-bench" to lend a hand or give advice). There is an interesting nearly violent encounter between Der and Tiurin toward the end of the story, about which later. Shukhov and/or the narrator often point out how, as you go higher up in the camp hierarchy, the laziness, ineptness, inhumanity, or corruption increases. Is this a way of saying what Lord Acton once said: "Power corrupts but absolute power corrupts absolutely"? Acton was speaking of political power in the nation, but is not Solzhenitsyn using the camp to make larger statements?

Shukhov or his narrator makes a number of assertions about his fellows, his supervisors, or the work they are performing at the power-station construction site. The two Estonians in the 104th, for example, prompt Shukhov to think that "every nation has its bad ones, but among all the Estonians he had ever known, he had never met a bad one." For the most part, Solzhenitsyn's characters who are of non-Russian nationality tend to be better-than-average sorts, although there are exceptions - the Moldavian (who acted as a spy against his own men), for example. The deaf Senka is at the site, too. Sometimes he appears to be staring off into space, his head cocked to one side in deaf oblivion - "poor devil," Shukhov remarks of him more than once. Deaf or not, Senka nevertheless knows what's going on, often better than those whose hearing is perfect. This is an interesting point made by Solzhenitsyn, that whatever is taking place in the camps is so obvious that even a deaf person could apprehend the pettiness, the corruption, the essentially inhumane social order represented by the System.

The man whom Shukhov tends most to respect as a fellow-worker (zeks are not permitted to use the word "comrade," even loosely, as it used to be applied to a close friend, without the Communist overtone) is the Lithuanian, KILGAS. They had worked on previous days as a carpenter-and-mason team. Kilgas takes pride in his work, as does Ivan Denisovich, and he knows how to be proudly resourceful on occasion. He also knows how to "scrounge" a little extra roofing felt from a neighboring project so that his and Shukhov's job can be done better. Incidentally, the scrounging from other work teams is an illustration of how little "collectivism" obtains at the camp, as well as outside the camp in normal Soviet life. Each work team takes all it can get, in order to earn better rations, do a better job in general to boost its standing, etc., without the slightest thought for the "whole," in the sense of e pluribus unum (the single whole made out of the many).

The narrator also comments on snowstorms, which are of vital concern to everyone anywhere east of the Ural Mountains. A true blizzard "is of no use to anyone." And yet, "the zeks loved snowstorms, even prayed for them.... Let the stuff come! A really huge snowfall!" They wanted a blizzard even though it meant that no flour for bread would be delivered, and that they would have to stay locked in their barracks during such a storm: "Prisoners could get lost somewhere between the barracks and the mess hall [if they were permitted out]... No one would care if a zek froze himself to death, but if he tried to escape, that was another matter. There had been instances where...." The author employs the snowstorm commentary to show how desperate the prisoners' lot could be - that they would pray for a snowstorm (buran), even if they would have to be confined indoors during it. That also meant no work out in the cold. What strikes you is that zeks would actually attempt to go over the hill even in such weather, the only kind of weather, in fact in which the attempt would be worth a try, although those who tried it, observes the narrator, "didn't get very far." The watchtowers, the guards with machine guns-it wasn't easy. The snowstorm commentary also illustrates the point that miracles do not save.

The task at the work site on this particular day consists in weather-proofing the machine room of the plant at the site. Tiurin explains that the three large windows will have to be boarded up since they do not keep out the cold. "You," he says, "will have to figure out what to board them up with."

This is where Shukhov and Kilgas, the carpenter-and-mason team, start figuring. Shukhov's trowel is as dear to him as his spoon. He "lifted" the best trowel in the area from the tool room. Trowels disappeared often and brick would have to be laid without them, so Shukhov hid his in a mass of brick and mortar. Kilgas and Shukhov go out to find the roofing felt, Kilgas joking off and on ("You'd be funny too if you were in his boots" - Kilgas ate well, got two food packages a month from the outside). They observe a group of men engaged in meaningless work, and practically freezing besides: "If the powers-that-be had any sense, would they send men to work chopping away at the ground with pickaxes in cold like this?" Kilgas remarks to "Vanya" (Ivan).

They make off with the roll of felt, to be used to caulk the boarded-up window frames, making sure that the civilian supervisor Der, the "bastard," and Shkuropatenko, old "stork legs," did not see them. Then, they head for the area where they will get the blocks and mortar. They encounter brak, defective mechanisms or articles which are common among Soviet consumer goods within the state-plan network. One "reject" is a mechanical lift-its power motor was burned out and no one had bothered to repair it. The other was the trough for mixing mortar, which had fallen apart. The men go to work repairing the trough, installing a stove pipe over the source of heat (which served the double purpose of mixing the cement as well as keeping the men "warm" in the machine room), the latter being Ivan's job. To repair the wooden trough, planks had to be taken cannibal-like from part of the scaffolding within the construction. After the scaffolding was removed, "You'd have to be alert, lest you fall over the edge," since the machine room is on the second floor.

There is a moving description of the building which is under construction and the relationship to it by the men of the 104th:

"... The unfinished structure [power station] stood in the snow like a gray skeleton, abandoned. But now the 104th work team had arrived on the scene. And what kept their spirits up? Empty bellies held in with belts made of rope! A vicious cold! No cozy corner! No warm fire! But the 104th had arrived - and life had returned to the building."

The various tasks performed by the men of the 104th are described in great detail by the narrator-author. In the bustle of activity, we sense the devotion to the job, a kind of stolid momentum impelling the men to make the best of what they're doing. Ivan Denisovich, for example, has only "one idea-to fix the bend in the stove pipe and suspend it so that it won't emit smoke."

The youthful Gopchik is introduced at this point in the narrative. Shukhov's own child had died young and Gopchik reminds him of him. "[Gopchik] was like a lovable little calf who fawned on everybody." Although only in his teens, Gopchik, a Ukrainian, had been arrested for carrying milk to a band of anti-Soviet deserters in World War I commanded by Bendera; his term in the camp was exactly like that of a full-grown adult. Gopchik wants Shukhov to cast him a spoon like Shukhov's. Gopchik, as "nimble as a squirrel," performs various hazardous tasks, like crawling precariously along high beams to fasten the wire holding the stove pipe. Like a baby calf he might be, but he is also cunning: "He always ate the contents of his food packages alone, sometimes at night."

Finally, the truck carrying the cement blocks arrives and the laborious transfer-manually-of mortar and blocks to the second-floor machine room begins. No one, of course, instructed the men as to how they might transport these materials to the second floor. "Masons, let's give it the look-see," says Pavlo. They finally decide on a combination of heaving and carrying the blocks, which they thought would be quicker than toting them up the ramp leading to the second floor. The work preoccupies Shukhov so much that time passes quickly. But not like the years of one's term in the camps: "They never seemed to pass, the end never seemed to be in sight."

As the lunch break is approaching, an interesting conversation breaks out between Shukhov and "Captain" Buinovsky, formerly of the Soviet navy. On several occasions the two men have weighty conversations, first about the sun and then later about the moon. "The sun's at its highest point," remarks Ivan, "it must be noon."

"No way," the captain remarks. "If it's reached its zenith, it's not noon but 1 o'clock."

"What does that mean?" Shukhov asks. "Any old man knows that the sun is at its highest point at lunchtime."

"Old guys, maybe," the captain says sharply, "but since their day a new decree has been passed so that now the sun is at its highest point at 1 o'clock."

"Who issued that decree?"

"The Soviet Government!" Shukhov then thinks to himself, with a certain peasant ingenuousness, perhaps: "You mean to say that the very sun up in the sky obeys their decrees?" (This was not edited out in the Soviet version as it appeared in the November 1962 number of *Novy Mir*; for parts that were edited out, see my commentary below-A.L.W.)

On the other occasion when Ivan and the captain have a more or less weighty discussion, the topic is the moon. Later, in the evening when they are leaving the power-station construction site, the two men look at the moon newly risen and looking crimson. Here, the narrator observes (accurately, from a strictly astronomical point of view) that the moon had been higher at this same time on the preceding night. "Listen, captain," Ivan says, "where does this science of yours say the old moon goes?"

"What do you mean 'goes'?" the captain exclaims. "Such naivete I've never seen!"

Shukhov shook his head and laughed: "Well, if it's not visible, then how do you know it's really there?"

"Well, then, according to you," said the captain incredulously, "it's another moon that rises every month!"

"What's so strange about that?" asks Ivan Denisovich. "New persons are born every day. Why not a new-born moon every four weeks?"

"Phooey," comments the captain as he punctuates his exasperation by spitting. "I've never met such a stupid sailor as you in all my life. So, where do you think the old moon goes?"

"That's what I'm asking you. Where does it go?"

"No, you tell me!" says the captain sarcastically.

"In our village," Shukhov answers, "the people say that God crumbles the old moon into star fragments."

"They're savages!" exclaims the captain. "That one I've never heard. So you believe in God, Shukhov?" (In the Soviet version: lower-case g.)

"Why not? When you hear Him thunder, how can you not believe?"

"Why, then, does God do this?" the captain asks him.

"Do what?"

"Crumble the moon into stars. Why?"

"Well, can't you understand that? The stars fall now and then. The gaps they leave behind have to be replenished."

Just then a guard interrupts this "weighty" discussion to bellow: "Turn around, you slob, and get in line."

FUNCTION OF "MOON" DIALOGUE

The point of this dialogue between Ivan and the captain is to show the contrast between a man trained in the literal, scientific understanding of the moon, through the captain's training in navigation, and one who knows the moon only in a romantic, folk-peasant way. The reader is left with the impression that the romantic, Ivan Denisovich version is rather pleasing and satisfactory. One cannot help thinking, also, that in 1962, when *One Day* was published, the moon was fast on the way to being "colonized" and totally understood by human beings. This may have been one way that Solzhenitsyn expressed the disillusionment felt by so many when that lover's orb, that "piece of cheese," that mysterious and serene neighbor of the earth was dissected like a corpse, forever losing its remoteness, its ghostly-galleon quality so beloved of poets, lovers, and simple folk. The dialogue also reveals a sort of playful streak in the hero. At times, one does not know whether to take him seriously. In any case, the vaudevillian repartee, somewhat reminiscent of the 1920s American comedy team of Moran & Mack, ends abruptly, even comically, when the guard intrudes with his "Turn around, you slob ..." (In Moran & Mack, the two black-faced comics discuss endlessly whether white horses eat more than black ones. That can't be, says Moran. Why should the white horses eat more than the black horses? To which Mack responds, "The only way we could figure it out was that there were more of the white horses." "God," says Shukhov, "replenishes the gaps" left by falling stars; that's why he crumbles the old moon. Oh well, why not?)

When lunch time at the site arrives, it turns out that very little tangible work has been done all morning. Most of the time has been spent deciding how to do the job, repairing the stove pipe, the mortar trough, getting the roofing felt, etc. "They weren't paid for fixing the stoves," observes the narrator. But something had to be written into the work report filed at the end of each day. This was the work of Tiurin, but also of Tsezar

A word about Tsezar. He formerly worked in the Soviet movie industry, before getting into trouble. He is the nearest to being a "King Rat" in the whole group-two parcels a month, "he greased every palm that had to be, worked in the office in a cushy job as deputy to the work-norm inspector." He was "well-off." (He is cast in the movie as a heavily mustachioed, keen-eyed individual as played by the English actor Eric Thompson.) Tsezar will get into a discussion about Soviet movies, especially Sergei Eisenstein, at the drop of a hat. This happens twice in the story, once in the construction-site office and another time with the captain.

In the first discussion, the topic is Eisenstein's Ivan the Terrible. Tsezar remarks to "a stingy old twenty-five year termer" that he thinks Ivan showed Eisenstein's genius. "The dance done by Ivan's guards, the oprichniki [Ivan the Terrible's secret police]! The cathedral scene!"

"Rot!" remarks the old man. "It's all so arty and souped-up that there's nothing artistic about it. It's all spices and poppy seeds instead of good, old, honest bread. And then the underlying political idea is pernicious: the justification for [Stalin's] one-man tyranny. It is a mockery of the memory of three generations of Russian intellectuals."

"But what other treatment of the subject would have been permitted?"

"Permitted!!??? Ugh! How can you call him a genius? Rather, call him a lackey, say that he carried out orders like a dog. Geniuses do not adapt their treatments of a subject to the tastes of tyrants."

On the other occasion when Tsezar discusses Soviet films, again it's Eisenstein, this time the great film-director's movie, Potemkin. Now Tsezar spars with the captain. "The baby-carriage on the steps. Bumping down and down," Tsezar comments enthusiastically.

The captain objects: "Yes, but the scenes on board [the Potemkin] seem somewhat artificial" (literally, puppet-like-kukol'naya).

"Well, maybe we have been spoiled by up-to-date camera technique."

"Those maggots crawling around on the meat," observes the captain, "they look more like angleworms. They couldn't have actually been like that!"

"Let 'em bring meat like that here to the camp instead of that fish they feed us. Let 'em dump it right into the pot. We would be..."

Again, a discussion is interrupted. This time by the roaring of prisoners: the Moldavian spy has held up the column because he stayed behind. Apparently, he had fallen asleep. "Ass! Louse! Pig!" the prisoners shout at him.

To return to the work site: Afternoon comes and the workers are at their various tasks. Der appears. Is he going to lend his usual useless advice to the men? He thinks he's an engineer. But the narrator observes: "Let a man build a whole house with his own hands before he starts calling himself an engineer." Der spots the filched roofing felt and warns that this could mean the guardhouse for the culprits who took it. Turning to Tiurin, whom it is unwise to get rough with, Der warns, "You could get a third term for this."

This confrontation between a representative of the higher camp administration (Der) and the squad leader Tiurin affords Solzhenitsyn the opportunity to comment on the split loyalty of work teams and camp. Tiurin, of course, defends the filching of roofing felt; he will not be treated like a pawn by the higher-ups. Tiurin gets so mad that he makes a move in Der's direction. Der gets the point and retreats when Tiurin barks at him: "If you utter one word about this, you bloodsucker, it'll be your last day on earth. Just remember that." Just before he leaves the machine room altogether, Der has to get in a dig at Ivan Denisovich - "Why are you using such a thin layer of mortar?" As Der descends the ramp, Tiurin yells after him that he had better get the motorized lift repaired: "What do you take us for, a bunch of work horses?"

ATTITUDE TOWARD STATE PROPERTY

At this point, with the mention again of the lift, the narrator comments on Soviet brak. He notes that zeks are careless with the machinery, sometimes actually wrecking it, not apparently by way of sabotage, just from thoughtlessness and not caring. (This writer saw a bulldozer being stored under a bridge for the weekend on his visit to Moscow. The bull-dozer had been left half-submerged in the river, as water seaped into some of the movable parts of the transmission and the engine. An example of negligence on the part of workers who seemed to care little about the maintenance of the State's equipment.)

As the workday grinds to an end-10 hours or longer in duration-Ivan Denisovich rushes to complete a section of wall that he had been building. He has had an excellent rhythm going with deaf Senka: mortar, block; mortar, block. He can't stop. "Finish, fuck you!" shouts Senka. "Let's get the hell out of here!" The guards would send the dogs after them if they didn't make assembly to re-group for the return trip "home." Rushing to make assembly, Shukhov nevertheless takes a few moments to stand back and survey his job: "Ah! Straight and level. His hands were as young as ever."

The zeks regroup-always moving forward in groups of fives (an effective procedure visually when it was done in the movie of *One Day*). As each quintet of zeks was called, they moved a few paces forward, like intelligent animals.

A delay sets in and the columns do not move off. Fifteen minutes, a half hour…it is biting cold as they stand in the pitch darkness. What's holding up the show? As everyone wonders and waits impatiently, the narrator comments on the firewood trick. It seems that each zek, if he can, tries to smuggle a few sticks of firewood to take back to the barracks. Everyone that does this knows that spot-checking along the way, and especially back at base, will result in the wood being seized. But it is a sort of charade-like so many other games played by zeks and guards-by which guards acquire some wood, while letting some get through intentionally so as not to discourage the smuggling activity altogether; otherwise, the guards wouldn't get any wood at all in this manner. The zeks calculated that some wood, at least, got through. The stealing of socialist property? Yes, but then both sides in the "racket" profited. (There have been any number of criminal cases in Soviet law where the stealing of public property benefited a number of interests, both administrative or managerial as well as the perpetrators. Universal "winking" at the practice may prevent exposure of the crime, but a prosecutor's office here or there sometimes crashes through, breaking the chain of mutual profiteering.)

What held up the columns was the absence of the Moldavian, the "Rumanian spy" (he had apparently spied against Russia in the service of Fascist Rumania). The Moldavian was continuing his spying activities in the camp, not for the zeks, but against them. When he finally appears, the zeks shout the worst imaginable obscenities at him, Shukhov joining in.

Just before Shukhov had left the site, he had found a hack-saw blade on the ground. Figuring that it could be of some use later on, he concealed it in his clothing. As he marches back to the camp, he remembers that he still has it. Once at the camp gates, Ivan realizes he will have to do something about the hack-saw blade. For a moment he forgets that he has it, as Tsezar lets him go at the head of the line so that Ivan can get to the post office to get Tsezar's package, with its aromatic tobacco, et al. With only a few zeks ahead of him until he himself is frisked, Shukhov remembers to his horror that the incriminating blade is on his person - an infraction which would mean solitary. Still, it was a pity to throw it away. In the very last few seconds, he conceals it in one of his mittens. There is a tension-ridden scene - and a beautifully written one-during which the guard, an older man whom Shukhov has moved toward intentionally (maybe he will be a don't-give-a-damn type, unlike a younger guard), frisks him up and down. He starts in on one of the mittens, but he never gets to the second, "loaded" mitten for someone calls to the old guard to hurry up. Shukhov is let through hack-saw blade and all. The narrator describes the return to camp of Shukhov and all the toiling zeks as follows:

"All those zeks, passing through the gates like soldiers returning home from a victorious campaign. They looked tensed up, seasoned in battle, self-confident. 'Make way for us,' they seemed to be saying."

As he waits in line to get Tsezar's package, Ivan Denisovich recalls that he had told his wife not to bother to send him packages. It wasn't worth the effort. Postal inspectors at the camp would open the packages, snitching their contents, and if they didn't do that, they would demand something in return from the zek to whom they gave the package. Each camp, after all, had its share of a black market, not unlike the situation on the other side of the barbed wire in the planned but often chronically unplanned economy, with its shortages and its brak. Other zeks may get their butter, or sugar for sweetening their tea in supreme luxury, or whatever. But as for Ivan Denisovich, he only wants to get the mess hall in time for the gruel - "It's only half as good cool as it is when eaten hot." Just before leaving the package line, Shukhov learns that another Sunday will be "stolen" from the zeks: the next "free day" (Sunday) is to become a workday. They'd always think of some reason or other for robbing the prisoners of one day-off a week: fixing the bathhouse, de-bugging bed bunks, or even re-checking your "mug" with your official photo. "Nothing seems to get the authorities' goat quicker than zeks resting quietly after breakfast." Or enjoying one free day a week.

After delivering Tsezar his package, Ivan hurries back to the barrack. He goes right to his mattress to make sure that the remaining half of dearly-prized bread has not been discovered - no, it's safe and sound, sewn into the hard-packed mattress. Then he rushes off to the mess hall.

IMPACT ON READER

There is a description of the mess-hall orderly, The Gimp. A prisoner himself, and like the cooks, this mess-hall orderly was treated with kid gloves: e.g., his number is written small, always an advantage since you cannot be spotted so easily. The

Gimp has a card-file memory for people, especially those with a little more "drag" than the rest. He carries a big club and speaks abusively to the men. Getting into the mess hall for the evening meal is far rougher and fiercer than at the morning meal. In fact, during the story, it becomes obvious that as night falls and that one day ends, all the various deprivations and repressions become more intense. It is part of the dialectics of labor-camp life; it also impacts the reader with the latent thought, "Good heavens! All this starts up anew the next day!" In fact, the author helps the reader in this fantasy when he has the narrator say: "It may get as low as - 40 degree Centigrade toward morning." The sky was clear and the moon shone starkly white, "as if chiseled out of stone."

At night, the men are fed according to the kind and the amount of work done during the day. Some received 12 oz. (like Shukhov), some fewer. After skirmishing with the mess-hall orderlies over the number of bowls for the 104th, Shukhov and his colleagues settle down to the studious devouring of their evening meal. "The stomach is a beast; it forgets how well you treated it at the last meal." Finishing the meal, Ivan licks his bowl and his spoon dry and returns his well-tooled eating implement to the inside of his boot.

Back at the barracks, there is a discussion of the Korean War (1950-1953). At the time of the story (1951) this war is in progress and some zeks are wondering aloud if the Chinese will join in the conflict (they did). The narrator notes meanwhile, as tobacco is being passed around, that at the "special" (political) camps, "you could let off steam." At the Ust-Izhma camp for "criminals," where Ivan Denisovich had formerly "sat," you were much more restricted than here. In Ust-Izhma, in the north, "All you had to do was whisper something-like there was a shortage of matches - and you'd be put in the guardhouse, or you'd have another 10 years added on to your term. Here, you could shout out anything from the upper bunks. The stool pigeons didn't pass it on, and the security boys didn't care anymore." At one point, a prisoner refers to the "whiskered old scoundrel" (Stalin: "Do you think he would ever take pity on you? Why he wouldn't trust his own mother!" A fragment of a conversation taking place between some zeks, used by the author to demonstrate the point about the outspokenness of camps for "politicals."

CONTRAST BETWEEN IVAN AND TSEZAR

Toward the end of the story, there is an interesting observation made of Tsezar by Shukhov; it recalls the point made by the critic Lopukhina-Rodzyanko about the contrast between the main character and Tsezar. "Despite the high opinion he had of himself," Shukhov thinks in relation to Tsezar, "he didn't know anything about life." Shukhov feels sorry for him: Tsezar has received so many goodies mailed from outside that he will be unable to conceal them all. He cannot carry them to roll-call-400 zeks would roar their heads off; the "lot" would get stolen if it were left in the barracks. Although Tsezar has obviously enjoyed and encouraged the sending of packages to him, his greed will likely get him into trouble, or at least prove the point that this temptation should be resisted. Still, Ivan, who gets no packages and who gets along without them, pities Tsezar and advises him to carry out a small ruse whereby he could keep his extra food. Tsezar later thanks his colleague with a formal "Thank you, Ivan Denisovich."

Retiring to his bunk at the end of the one day, Ivan says, "Glory be to God! One more day finished without spending the night in solitary, thanks be to Thee." Alyosha comments to Ivan that he should pray. "Well, you see, Alyosha, it's like this," replies Ivan, "prayers are like written grievances. Either they never get to those to whom they are addressed or they are sent back with 'rejected' scrawled across them." (Again, resist the temptation to expect God to work miracles.)

"But you see, Ivan Denisovich," pleads Aloysha, "this happens because you don't pray often enough, and when you do, you pray badly. You don't really try... A person with true faith can move mountains."

"That's nonsense," says Ivan. "Have you ever seen a mountain move? Well, to tell you the truth, I've never even seen a mountain. But take you-you've prayed in the Caucasus Mountains with all those Baptists of yours. Did you make a single mountain move?" Alyosha replies, with a certain Biblical wisdom, that the Baptists, who always got 25 years for their "heresy," never prayed for miracles or material benefits. "The Lord commanded us to pray only for our daily bread." To which the practical Ivan replies, "Our bread ration, don't you mean?" intentionally or unintentionally misunderstanding the point made by the good Alyosha the Baptist. Along with their religious discussion, Shukhov brings up the subject of the venality of village Russian Orthodox priests, one of whom he knows pays alimony to three different women in as many villages. (Solzhenitsyn himself is of the Orthodox faith.)

"Don't talk to me about such priests," Alyosha protests. "The Orthodox have departed from Scripture. The only reason they are not in prison is that their faith is not firm enough."

Shukhov notes to himself that Alyosha's face has a serene quality leaving no doubt that he is actually happy in prison.

"Alyosha, it works out all right for you, you see. Jesus Christ wanted you to sit in prison and so here you are, 'sitting' for His sake. But for whose sake am I here? Because we were not ready for war in '41? For that? Was that my fault?" (Recall that Shukhov was falsely accused of spying for the Germans after he and a group of men are captured at the very start of the war and then escape back to their own lines.)

Suddenly the call goes up, "Second count!" Another roll-call, although some men are already dozing off. "Damn them!" mutters Shukhov who has almost dropped off to sleep. The recount is held indoors. "Come on, come on!" growl the guards. "Do you want to be carried out of your bunks, you shit?" Once the recount is over and the guards have left, Shukhov thinks to himself that Alyosha is so gentle to everyone but never expects or gets anything in return. Shukhov hands Alyosha a biscuit which had been given him by Tsezar. "But you've got nothing for yourself," remarks Alyosha, reluctant to take the biscuit. "Eat it," says Shukhov.

And then come the memorable final lines of *One Day in the Life of Ivan Denisovich*:

"Shukhov went off to sleep feeling completely contented. Many good things had come his way this day: he had not been put in solitary; his work team had not been sent to the Socialist Community Center; he had pilfered a bowl of kasha at supper; the team leader had cleverly 'adjusted' the work-norms; he had built a wall and enjoyed doing it; he had smuggled through the hack-saw blade; he had earned a favor from Tsezar and bought some tobacco. And he hadn't gotten ill and had risen above it.

"The day passed without a dark cloud. It was almost a happy day.

"There were 3,653 such days left in his term, from the reveille clanging of the rail to the last clanging at lights-out.

"The three extra days were for leap years …"

LANGUAGE AND STYLE, TRANSLATION

LANGUAGE AND STYLE OF "ONE DAY"

Alexander Solzhenitsyn's style of writing is economical and unornamental. This is particularly true of *One Day*. This would seemingly cause little difficulty in translating *One Day* were it not for the great amount of prison jargon contained in the dialogues and discussion of life in the camp.

The author's motto might well be, "wie es eigentlich gewesen," or "tell it like it is." In believing as he does in honest **realism** and not the propaganda slogan of "socialist realism," Solzhenitsyn wishes to render the real-life situations he describes in so many of his writings-but especially in *One Day*-in real-life language. The author did not have to use any glossaries of prison argot, although the translator must; Solzhenitsyn simply drew on his own 8-years' experience in corrective labor camps.

ARTISTIC USE OF BLUNT LANGUAGE

Many "unprintable" Russian words turn up in *One Day*, as it was first published in *Novy Mir*. Words like khub kren, yebat', govno and der'mo, khui, pizda, etc., would make Beelzebub himself blush, but since they are part of a zek's vocabulary, they appear in the novella. In the half-dozen extant English translations of the work, these words are rendered with the frankness of a Henry Miller novel. In Solzhenitsyn's case, the reader gets the impression that far from wishing to be shocking or sensational, the author has used these obscenities to show how debased humans can become. In any case, most of the smutty language comes out of the mouths of the camp authorities. This undoubtedly is the author's way of illustrating the source of the debasement, debasement not only of language but of human beings.

In a brilliantly written essay, L. Rzhevsky notes how the blunt language lends an "immediacy and sincerity of tone" to the story (in *Tvorets i Podvig: Ocherki po Tvorchestvu Aleksandra Solzhenitsyna* [*The Artist and His Accomplishments: Notes on the Writings of Alexander Solzhenitsyn*], Possev-Verlag, Frankfurt/Main). "The simplicity and credibility of the story" are enhanced by this device, whether the scene be in the barracks, at the construction site, or during the friskings and body counts. Professor Christopher Moody speaks in his book (see Bibliography) of the author's own familiarity with Russian peasant life; he has learned how to convey the "idiom of the common people." Solzhenitsyn studied philological texts (such as Dal's famous dictionary) to verify expressions that he heard, and he took copious notes, as Dostoyevsky had done before him, as found in Dostoyevsky's *Diary of a Writer*. Some of Solzhenitsyn's proverbs appear to be lifted from Dal. Moody cites and proverb found in *One Day*, "How can you expect a man who is warm to understand a man who is cold" (from the infirmary scene where Shukhov is commenting about Kolya upon leaving the hospital). But the Dal original renders it, "A man who is satisfied cannot understand one who is hungry." So in these and other cases, Solzhenitsyn did not reproduce Dal but only adapted Dal to his own purposes. Moody notes also Solzhenitsyn's folk-tale (skaz) flavor. He cites the "stitch-stitch-stitch" line when Shukhov is sewing into his mattress the remaining half of a piece of bread; one might also mention the top-top, skrip-skrip onomatopoeia, which is Russian folk speech.

Moody also notes how Solzhenitsyn's descriptions do not retard the pace of *One Day*. The story's tempo is not slowed down, "nor does the rhythm become monotonous." The wealth of detail is combined with the lively pace of narration in which broken phrases, a wealth of emotionally-colored interrogatory and exclamatory figures, expressive parenthetical words and phrases, ellipses and unusual word order are used to best advantage.

"SKAZ" STORY-TELLING

As to the folk-tale manner of *One Day*, Professor Moody and others note how Solzhenitsyn fits into the Russian tradition of Pilniak, Zamyatin, and Babel, not to mention prerevolutionary writers like Leskov and Gogol. In the skaz, the story-teller, or narrator, is one the same level as the main characters in the story. He think their thoughts and uses their language. The skaz strategy for telling the story permits the author to tailor in a great deal of "local color," to lend the story an eye-witness flavor through the making of astute, sometimes humorous and sardonic observations or commentaries. The narration in *One Day* permits the reader along with the author vicariously to dart in and out of the situations or conversations, as if he were there, both participating as well as describing goings-on. *One Day's* narration is enhanced by the fact that the language is at times simple and slangy and full of zek argot. The "darting-in-and-out" technique is accomplished by Solzhenitsyn without establishing any clear dividing line between Shukhov's speaking and the author's speaking. Moody notes that the voices "interchange so imperceptibly that the reader is often uncertain which is speaking." At times it will necessitate extreme care on the part of the reader to disentangle an unspoken monologue of Shukhov from an exterior observation made by the author through the unseen narrator, who is in the third person.

Moreover, the Shukhov himself is speaking, in a dialogue for example, it is sometimes difficult to know whether he is speaking to us, the readers, or to another character in the dialogue. At this juncture, the author, via the narrator, may step in to wrap up a scene with a comment or observation.

In brief, the author has employed a number of techniques to achieve his overall strategy in *One Day*. Above all, he wants to tell us the truth in the manner in which we are generally acquainted with raw truth: as a blunt, lopsided thing which we have no other choice but to accept. Avoiding as he does ornamentation or lengthy sentences and description (in the Dickensian or Dostoyevskian manner), Solzhenitsyn accomplishes a stoic austerity which somehow suits the equally stark scenes, lean figures, and clean-shaven heads of the zeks etched against the bleak white background of the Siberian camp.

OMITTED SECTIONS FROM THE ORIGINAL "ONE DAY"

Late in 1974, at the time of his forcible banishment from the USSR, Solzhenitsyn revealed that parts of *One Day in the Life of Ivan Denisovich* had been censored before it appeared in *Novy Mir*. Subsequent translations of *One Day* from the *Novy Mir* original, therefore, have lacked these omitted sections. To date, then, no completely uncensored version of *One Day* has appeared in

English although the uncensored version is available in Russian (YMCA press Paris edition of *One Day* dated 1973).

For example, there are a number of instances in the uncensored version where Shukhov refers to his former life in the village before the war and his arrest. At one point, he compares the way the zeks' boots have to be returned to a whole pile of boots at the end of the day to the "way they drove horses into the kolkhoz" (during collectivization); this was struck out of the *Novy Mir* manuscript by the Soviet censor. The uncensored version contains some frank remarks in letters to Shukhov from his wife, e.g.: "His old lady wrote him once that all those who did not fulfill the work norm would be clapped into prison. But for some reason the law has not been enforced." The sentenced about "women keeping the kolkhoz going since the 1930s" was left intact by the censor except for a phrase which read, "... who were driven into the kolkhoz since the 1930s," and "... when they [the women] fell dead, kolkhoz would also kick the bucket." Some of Tiurin's reminiscences about life during collectivization and after were scissored out by the censors. In them Tiurin recounts the manhunt for "kulaks," meaning peasants of modest or better means who wished to retain their private property as independent peasants. In the uncensored version, Tiurin remarks: "They had taken away my father already. Mother and the kids were still waiting to be deported. The village authorities have already been sent a telegram about me and they were looking for me. We were shaking all over. We turned out all the lights in the house and sat down on the floor under the window so that if the Bolshevik activists who were running around the village should peer in, they would not see us." Other excised passages which the Soviet censor would not permit to be printed relate to the Soviet bureaucracy, the forcible annexation of parts of Poland, the harsh treatment accorded Russian returnees from German POW camps after the war, and other sensitive areas pertaining to Soviet history. The censor was especially sensitive to the *One Day* narrator's tendency to speak of possible revenge for the inhumane treatment of zeks or even of Soviet citizens. For example, Shukhov thinks about Der (the civilian bureaucrat at the work site), "Here he is again. One should get the blood of this bastard ... [Once] three such types were knifed to death and the camp became a different place ... If only the zeks would not backbite each other so much ... the authorities had no power over them." All of this was censored. Defiance on the part of the oppressed is not permissible reading!

One critic who has closely examined the unedited, uncensored version of *One Day* has remarked: "[Omissions and] additions were deliberately made in order to change the meaning of a given situation.... For example, when the former navy captain, Buinovsky, gets furious about the guards taking away his second undershirt, he shouts to Volkovoi: "You are not Soviet people!" The censor added another short sentence: "You are not Communists." The obvious meaning is that real Communists would not treat their prisoners this way; therefore, one cannot really blame the Communists, or the Communist system. Undoubtedly, the uncensored *One Day* in a harder-hitting book than the censored, English version most people must read at present. Some of the "stoical," almost submissive qualities of Ivan Denisovich are the work of the censor, not the author Alexander Solzhenitsyn.

A NOTE ON TRANSLATIONS

"[Translations] are one of my chief worries in the West," Alexander Solzhenitsyn told a group of newsmen in December 1974. "In some countries I have found the translations of my books in a dreadful state." In his remarks, the author seemed mainly to have the works *Cancer Ward* and *The First Circle* on his mind (he mentioned the first) when it came to inept translations. He has never commented on the state of the art as relates to *One Day*.

The four major English translations of *One Day* are by Thomas P. Whitney, Ralph Parker, Gillon Aitken, and Max Hayward and Ronald Hingley. In the opinion of the writer of this critical commentary, shared by a number of native speakers of Russian, the Hayward-Hingley translation belongs at the top of the list. There are several reasons for this. Hayward and Hingley avoid two extremes: producing an English translation which is flavored too much with English or American-English slang or expressions, thus losing the Russian coloring; or on the other hand, producing one in which the original Russian has been translated laboriously and too literally. The translators were able to remain loyal to the original while rendering the dialogue, slang, proverbs, etc., in language which would be meaningful for English-speakers. Moreover, the accuracy of their translation is outstanding.

Among the weakness of the others are: overly Americanized (Whitney); somewhat stuffily Briticistic (Aitken); Briticisms and some inattention to the original Russian (Parker).

Without going into boring detail (for the general reader) about particular strengths and weaknesses in the four translations, one or two examples will suffice to make the point. The minor character Shkuropatenko is described by the author as dolgovyaziy (longlegged, like a stork); by one of the translators, he is a "goose egg." When the author described the two kinds of work a zek must perform-one for people who care, the other for people who do not know the difference or do not care-he says that work performed for the second type of person is done pokazukhu, "for show." In one of the translations, this expression was rendered "eye-wash" while in another, "pretend to [do good work]." Hayward and Hingley rendered it, "go through the motions." This is by far the best, but this writer humbly suggests, "put on a show," "do it for show," or "put on an act" as three alternative possibilities. The outdoor temperature is invariably given in centigrade (Celsius) in the translations. If the reader wishes to know what this would be in Fahrenheit, he will have to convert the centigrade readings to Fahrenheit by multiplying the Celsius temperature by 9, dividing by 5 and then adding 32, being careful, of course, of plus or minus signs! For example, the temperature in the morning in *One Day* was -27 1/2 degrees C, or about -17 degrees F. Several other minor differences in the spelling of the first names of some of the characters may be found between the translations. For example, Hayward and Hingley prefer "Caesar" to "Tsezar" for Tsezar Markovich; Buynovsky to Buinovsky; Tyurin to Tiurin; Fetyukov to Fetiukov, etc.

In his 1974 interview, Solzhenitsyn added that he thought translations would improve if translators were only paid more for their services. The author remarked that he wished to set up a system whereby the interests of translators could be defended in their contract negotiations with publishers. "I wish to make it a condition for publishing my books that the translators will be well paid," he said.

MAJOR WORKS BY ALEXANDER SOLZHENITSYN

One Day in the Life of Ivan Denisovich (a novel) *Matryona's Place* (a story) *An Incident at Krechetovka Station* (a story) *For the Good of the Cause* (a story) *The First Circle* (a novel) *Cancer Ward* (a novel) "Zakhar-Kalita" (a short story) *Feast of the Conquerors* (a play) "The Right Hand" (a story) *A Candle in the Wind* (a play) "The Easter Procession" (a story) "Answer to Three Students" (an essay) *The Love-Girl and The Innocent* (a play) *August 1914* (a novel) *Gulag Archipelago* (a novel) *From under the Rubble* (manifesto)

Various "prose poems" and essays, letters, and interviews.

STUDY GUIDE BIBLIOGRAPHY

BOOKS

Bjorkegren, Hans. *Aleksandr Solzhenitsyn: A Biography*, The Third Press, Joseph Okpaku Publishing Company, Inc., New York, 1972.

Burg, David and George Feifer. *Solzhenitsyn*, Stein and Day Publishers, New York, 1972.

Dostoyevsky, Fyodor. *Notes from the House of the Dead*, Dutton, New York, 1974.

Galler, Meyer and Harlan E. Marquess. *Soviet Prison Camp Speech: A Survivor's Glossary*, The University of Wisconsin Press, 1972.

Hardwood, Ronald. *The Making of* "One Day in the Life of Ivan Denisovich," Ballantine Books, New York, 1971.

Hayward, Max and Edward L. Crowley (eds). *Soviet Literature in the Sixties*, Frederick A. Praeger, Publisher, New York, 1964.

Labedz, Leopold (ed). *Solzhenitsyn: A Documentary Record*, Harper & Row, New York, 1970.

Lopukhina-Rodzyanko, T. *Dukhovniye Osnovy Tvorchestva Solzhenitsyna* (*The Spiritual Roots of Solzhenitsyn's Writings*), Possev-Verlag, Frankfurt/Main, 1974.

Lukacs, Georg. *Solzhenitsyn*, The MIT Press, Cambridge, Mass., 1971.

Medvedev, Zhores. *Ten Years after Ivan Denisovich*, Alfred A. Knopf, New York, 1973

Muller, Herbert J. *The Spirit of Tragedy*, Alfred, A. Knopf, New York, 1956.

Rothberg, Abraham. *The Heirs of Stalin Dissidence and the Soviet Regime: 1953-1970*, Cornell University Press, Ithaca-London, 1972.

Rzhevsky, L. *Tvorets i Podvig: Ocherki po Tvorchestvu Aleksandra Solzhenitsyna* (*The Artist and His Accomplishments: Notes on the Writings of Alexander Solzhenitsyn*), Possev-Verlag, Frankfurt/Main, 1972.

Solzhenitsyn, Aleksandr. *Odin Den' Ivana Denisovicha* (*One Day in the Life of Ivan Denisovich*), *Novy Mir*, November 1962.

_____, et al., *From under the Rubble*, Little, Brown and Company, New York, 1975.

Weeks, Albert L. *Andrei Sakharov and the Soviet Dissidents*, Monarch Press, Simon & Schuster, Inc., New York 1975.

Williams, Raymund. *Modern Tragedy*, Stanford University Press, Stanford, 1966.

ARTICLES

Feifer, George. "Solzhenitsyn: Conscience of a Nation," *Reader's Digest*, September 1974.

Laber, Jeri. "The Real Solzhenitsyn," *Commentary*, May 1974.

Solzhenitsyn, Alexander. "Press Conference," Feb. 14, 1975, *Radio Liberty Research Bulletin Supplement*, Feb. 14, 1975.

_____"Press Conference," Dec. 12, 1974, *Radio Liberty Research Bulletin Supplement*, June 3, 1974.

_____"The Big Losers in the Third World War," *The New York Times*, June 22, 1975.

_____"Peace and Violence," *The New York Times*, Sept. 13, 1973.

EXPLORE THE ENTIRE LIBRARY OF BRIGHT NOTES STUDY GUIDES

From Shakespeare to Sinclair Lewis and from Plato to Pearl S. Buck, The Bright Notes Study Guide library spans hundreds of volumes, providing clear and comprehensive insights into the world's greatest literature. Discover more, faster with the Bright Notes Study Guide to the classics you're reading today.

See the entire library of available
Bright Notes guides at **BrightNotes.com**

Available in print and digital wherever books are sold

IP INFLUENCE PUBLISHERS

www.ingramcontent.com/pod-product-compliance
Lightning Source LLC
LaVergne TN
LVHW011731060526
838200LV00051B/3136